PΓ405500

ANTHEM PUBLISHING

*Sermons of St. Bernard on*
*Advent & Christmas*

St. Bernard of Clairvaux

INCLUDES THE FAMOUS TREATISE ON THE
INCARNATION CALLED "MISSUS EST"

ANTHEM PUBLISHING
A Division of re:SOURCE DIGITAL PUBLISHING
Formatted and Printed in the United States of America
Digital edition also available.
ISBN: 9798692704481

*Compiled and translated at St. Mary's Convent, York, from the Edition (1508), in black-letter, of St. Bernard's Sermons and Letters*

**Nihil Obstat**.

HENRICUS G. S. BOWDEN,

Censor Deputatus.

**Imprimatur**.

EDM. CAN. SURMONT,

VICARIUS GENERALIS.

WESTMONASTERII,

*die 25 Octobris*, 1909.

# TABLE OF CONTENTS

# INTRODUCTION

**It** is a pleasure to write a few words of introduction to an admirable translation of some interesting "Sermons of St. Bernard" made by one of the Community of St. Mary's, York. The sermons are nineteen in number, and are all of them related to the mysteries of Advent and Christmas. Of the seven sermons, *De Adventu Domini*, printed in Dom Mabillon's edition of the saint's works, we have here the first two. Then follow the four homilies on the text *Missus est*, etc. This is the title that is generally given to these famous sermons, but the holy preacher himself intended them to be called *De laudibus Virginis Matris*, as we read in his letter to Peter the Deacon. Of the six discourses for the Vigil of Christmas, the translator has selected the first, the fourth, and the sixth. All the five sermons on Christmas Day are given. The volume ends with two on the Circumcision and three on the Epiphany.

These sermons are fully and conscientiously translated. A few omissions have been made—chiefly, it would seem, through sheer inability to present in an acceptable modern version all the devout and fanciful dealings of the holy Doctor with the text of the Scripture. St. Bernard knew St. Augustine well, and he had learnt this fashion of using Holy Scripture from him. St. Bernard's mind and heart were steeped in the Scriptures, and it comes natural to one to whom the text is so living and real to treat it as holding a lesson in every word and syllable. I have used the word "fanciful," but rather in the sense of imaginative fertility than of childish or mere poetic dreaminess. The Holy Spirit, as all Catholics believe, has a message for man in the Bible beneath and besides the letter. In general, it is the prerogative of the saints and doctors to discourse and reveal this mystical sense. This is the reason why the commentaries of holy men are so precious. For the exposition of a St. Augustine, a St. Gregory, or a St. Bernard is the expression of the interior illumination of a favoured soul, and it would be rash to doubt that such comments are, in a general sense, guided and "inspired" by the Author of the Scripture Himself. If, then, the translator of these sermons has found some passages too "quaint" to be reproduced, still, there is a sufficient number left to make it useful to remind the reader that he is here listening to one of the princes of the contemplative life, and that he should rather try to follow the idea than to criticize. No one can read St. Bernard with any profit or satisfaction who does not heartily accept him as a mystical expert in Holy Scripture. In one or two places considerable liberty has been taken with the text of the sermons. We are informed, in regard to the sermon on the Circumcision (p. 135), that this sermon has been combined with one on the same subject in the saint's commentary on the Canticle of Canticles. As the earlier discourse touches on the Holy Name, and as it is not, perhaps, one of St. Bernard's most striking utterances, it was a temptation not to be resisted to have recourse to the well-known Fifteenth Sermon on the Canticles, and to attach to the first the famous passages in which the Holy Name is compared to *Lux, Cibus, et Medicina*. This truly Bernardine outburst presents great difficulties to the translator, if the spirit and rhythm of the original are to be reproduced. It will be seen that the present translation is not unworthy of the original. I may, however, be permitted to say that, in the thrilling passage where the miracle wrought by the Holy Name on the cripple at the Gate of the Temple is described, I miss the *tanquam fulgur egrediens*—the comparison of Peter's utterance of that Name to a flash of lightning. The fine oratorical point which ends that passage—the healing of one cripple contrasted with the illumination of multitudes of blind—is left out. This kind of shortcoming rarely occurs in these pages, and is only an example of the excessive difficulty of rendering the exact rhetorical turn of a very vivid Latin into corresponding English.

St. Bernard's sermons were all delivered in the Chapter-house at Clairvaux. There can be no doubt that they were spoken in Latin, as we have them now. If the lay-brothers were present, they had to be content at the moment with picking up what they could, but we learn that at other times these discourses were repeated to the lay-brethren in French, or in the Romance tongue which was the precursor of modern French. We have a specimen of translation which must be almost contemporary, and possibly by St. Bernard himself, in a Paris manuscript quoted by Mabillon. The version shows that even an illiterate may have caught much of the sense of the spoken Latin. For example, in the sermon for Advent, the passage beginning, "Fugite superbiam, fratres mei, quæso, multum fugite," begins in Romance, "Por Deu, chier Friere, fuyez orgoil, et forment lo fuyez." St. Bernard's Latin style was much admired by the Humanists, such as Henry of Valois and Erasmus. The latter very acute critic says he was a born preacher, spirited, pleasing, and moving. We must remember that up to his twentieth year he had an excellent training in scholarship and divinity at Chatillon. His reading in both sacred and profane literature must have been very wide. He is well acquainted with theology, as one can see, for example, in his sermons on the Canticles, especially in Sermons 80 and 81, where he discourses on the image of God in the Word and in the soul of man, and on the simplicity of God, with a penetration not unworthy of St. Anselm. His knowledge of the Canon Law is shown in his most able treatise, addressed to Eugenius III., the fine book *De Consideratione*. It is true he never considered himself a student. He said that he learnt more from the "oaks and beeches" of the Cistercian solitude than from books or masters. What he thus learnt was the most precious part of what he has left us. But still, great Popes, like Alexander III. and Innocent III., have given him the title of Doctor, a title conferred upon him in a more liturgical way by Pope Pius IX. At what date he was first called the "Mellifluous" Doctor is a little uncertain. Theophilus Raynauld, who wrote in the fifteenth century, seems to be the first who records that name, but it carried too happy a description of his spirit not to be promptly taken up. It was Nicholas Faber, the tutor of Louis XIII., who called him the "Last of the Fathers."

Those who cannot read the "Sermons of St. Bernard" in the original may be strongly recommended to study them in this excellent translation. They will find the style, and even the matter, a little difficult. In a writer of the twelfth century there must be an idiom that is unfamiliar, and his subjects and his points will not be those of the books and preachers of our own times. But the reader will find in St. Bernard, as in all the Fathers, that steady, large, and almost unconscious exposition of Catholic faith in its widest sense, which the multiplication of religious books must always need as a corrective to limited views and one-sided enthusiasms. He will also, I do not doubt, appreciate the fire and piety of that great saint. The ardent devotion which marks every page of his sermons may not now be a novelty to Catholics, for a leader like St. Bernard makes his own spirit in this regard an inheritance of the whole Church, and we are all to a great extent thinking the devout thoughts and practising the elevations of the heart of which he gave the example. But it is always inspiring and stimulating to go to the fountain-head, and to study the very turns and expressions of such a master; and his touching piety, whenever he treats of the Word made flesh, or the Virgin-Mother, will always be more real to us and more edifying when we feel ourselves actually in his presence—the presence of one who was at once so heroic in his sanctity, and so great an historical figure in the twelfth century.

X J. C. H.

*November 5, 1909.*

*Sermons of St. Bernard on*
*Advent & Christmas*

---

St. Bernard of Clairvaux

INCLUDES THE FAMOUS TREATISE ON THE
INCARNATION CALLED "MISSUS EST"

WITH INTRODUCTION

BY THE

RIGHT REV. J. C. HEDLEY, O.S.B.

BISHOP OF NEWPORT

x

# 1
# ADVENT

# Sermons of St. Bernard

## SERMON I

## On The Advent of Our Lord and Its Six Circumstances

To-day we celebrate the beginning of Advent.

The name of this great annual commemoration is sufficiently familiar to us; its meaning may not be so well known.

When the unhappy children of Eve had abandoned the pursuit of things true and salutary, they gave themselves up to the search for those that are fleeting and perishable. To whom shall we liken the men of this generation, or to what shall we compare them, seeing they are unable to tear themselves from earthly and carnal consolations, or disentangle their minds from such trammels? They resemble the shipwrecked who are in danger of being overwhelmed by the waters, and who may be seen catching eagerly at whatever they first grasp, how frail soever it may be. And if anyone strive to rescue them, they are wont to seize and drag him down with them, so that not infrequently the rescuer is involved with them in one common destruction. Thus the children of the world perish miserably while following after transitory things and neglecting those which are solid and enduring, cleaving to which, they might save their souls. Of truth, not of vanity, it is said: "You shall know the truth, and the truth shall make you free."[1]

Do you, therefore, to whom as to little ones God has revealed things hidden from the wise and prudent, turn your thoughts with earnestness to those that are truly desirable, and diligently meditate on this coming of our Lord. Consider Who He is that comes, whence He comes, to whom He comes, for what end He comes, when He comes, and in what manner He comes. This is undoubtedly a most useful and praiseworthy curiosity, for the Church would not so devoutly celebrate the season of Advent if there were not some great mystery hidden therein.

Wherefore, in the first place, let us with the Apostle consider in astonishment and admiration how great He is Who comes. According to the testimony of Gabriel, He is the Son of the Most High, and consequently a coequal with Him. Nor is it lawful to think that the Son of God is other than coequal with His Father. He is coequal in majesty; He is coequal in dignity. Who will deny that the sons of princes are princes, and the sons of kings kings?

But how is it that of the Three Persons Whom we believe, and confess, and adore in the Most High Trinity, it was not the Father, nor the Holy Ghost, but the Son that became Man? I imagine this was not without cause. But "who hath known

---

[1] John 8:32

the mind of the Lord? Or who hath been his counsellor?"[2] Not without some most deep counsel of the Blessed Trinity was it decreed that the Son should become Incarnate. If we consider the cause of our exile, we may perchance be able to comprehend in some degree how fitting it was that our deliverance should be chiefly accomplished by the Son.

Lucifer, who rose brightly as the morning star, because he attempted to usurp a similitude with the Most High, and "it *was* thought robbery in him to equal himself with God,"[3] an equality which was the Son's by right, was cast down from heaven and ruined; for the Father was zealous for the glory of the Son, and seemed by this act to say: "Vengeance is mine, I will repay."[4] And instantly "I saw Satan as lightning falling from heaven."[5]

Dust and ashes, why art thou proud? If God spared not pride in His angels, how much less will He tolerate it in thee, innate corruption? Satan had committed no overt act, he had but consented to a thought of pride, yet in a moment, in the twinkling of an eye, he was irreparably rejected because, as the Evangelist says, "he stood not in the truth."[6]

Fly pride, my brethren, I most earnestly beseech you. "Pride is the beginning of all sin,"[7] and how quickly did it darken and overshadow with eternal obscurity Lucifer, the

---

[2] Romans 11:34
[3] Philippians 2:6
[4] Romans 12:9
[5] Luke 2:18
[6] John 8:44
[7] Ecclesiasticus 10:13

most bright and beautiful of the heavenly spirits, and, from not only an angel, but the first of angels, transform him into a hideous devil! Wherefore, envying man's happiness, he brought forth in him the evil which he had conceived in himself by persuading man that if he should eat of the forbidden tree he would become as God, having a knowledge of good and evil. Wretch! what dost thou promise, when thou knowest that the Son of God has the key of knowledge—yea, and is Himself the "key of David, that shutteth and no man openeth"[8]; that "in him are hidden all the treasures of the wisdom and knowledge of God"[9]? Wouldst thou, then, wickedly steal them away to give them to men?

You see, my brethren, how true is the sentence of our Lord, "The devil is a liar and the father of lies."[10] He was a liar in saying, "I will be like unto the Most High,"[11] and he was the father of lies when he breathed his spirit of falsity into man. "You will be as gods."[12] And wilt thou, O' man, "seeing the thief, run with him"[13]? You have heard, my brethren, what has been read this night from Isaiah. The Prophet says to the Lord, "Thy princes are faithless, companions of thieves," or, as another version has it, "disobedient companions of thieves."[14] In truth, Adam and Eve were disobedient companions of thieves, for, by the counsel of the serpent, or,

---

8 Revelation 3:7
9 Colossians 2:3
10 John 8:44
11 Isaiah 14:14
12 Genesis 3:5
13 Psalm 49:18
14 Isaiah 1:23

rather, of the devil in the serpent, they tried to seize upon what belonged by birthright to the Son of God. Nor did the Father overlook the injury, for the Father loveth the Son. He immediately took revenge on that same man, and let His hand fall heavily on us all, "for in Adam all have sinned,"[15] and in his sentence of condemnation we have shared.

What, then, did the Son do, seeing His Father so zealous for His glory, and for His sake sparing none of His creatures? "Behold," He says, "on My account My Father has ruined His creatures: the first of the angels aspired to My throne of sovereignty, and had followers who believed in him; and instantly My Father's zeal was heavily revenged on him, striking him and all his adherents with an incurable plague, with a dire chastisement. Man, too, attempted to steal from Me the knowledge which belongs to Me alone, and neither doth My Father show him mercy, nor doth His eye spare him. He had made two noble orders sharing His reason, capable of participating in His beatitude, angels and men; but behold, on My account He hath ruined a multitude of His angels and the entire race of men. Therefore, that they may know that I love My Father, He shall receive back through Me what in a certain way He seems to have lost through Me. 'It is on my account this storm has arisen; take me and cast me into the sea.'[16] All are envious of Me; behold I come, and will exhibit Myself to them in such a guise as that whosoever shall wish may become

---

[15] Romans 5:12
[16] Jonah 1:12

like to Me; whatsoever I shall do they may imitate, so that their envy shall be made good and profitable to them."

The angels, we know, sinned through malice, not through ignorance and frailty; wherefore, as they were unwilling to repent, they must of necessity perish, for the love of the Father and the honour of the King demand judgment. For this cause He created men from the beginning, that they might fill those lost places, and repair the ruins of the heavenly Jerusalem. For He knew "the pride of Moab, that he is exceedingly proud,"[17] and that his pride would never seek the remedy of repentance, nor, consequently, of pardon. After man's fall, however, He created no other creature in his place, thus intimating that man should yet be redeemed, and that he who had been supplanted by another's malice might still by another's charity be redeemed.

Be it so, dear Lord, I beseech Thee. Be pleased to deliver me, for I am weak. Like Joseph of old, I was stolen away from my country, and here without any fault was cast into a dungeon. Yet I am not wholly innocent, but innocent compared with him who seduced me. He deceived me with a lie: let the truth come, that falsehood may be discovered, and that I may know the truth, and that the truth may make me free. But to gain the freedom I must renounce the falsehood when discovered, and adhere to the known truth; otherwise the temptation would not be human, nor the sin a human sin, but diabolical obstinacy. To persevere in evil is the act of the

---

[17] Isaiah 16:6

devil, and those who persevere in evil after his example deservedly perish with him.

Behold, you have heard Who He is that comes; consider now whence and to whom He comes. He comes from the heart of God the Father to the womb of a virgin mother; He comes from the highest heaven to this low earth, that we whose conversation is now on earth may have Him for our most desirable companion. For where can it be well with us without Him, and where ill if He be present? "What have I in heaven, and besides Thee what do I desire upon earth? Thou art the God of my heart and the God that is my portion for ever"[18]; and "though I should walk in the midst of the shadow of death, I will fear no evil," if only "thou art with me."[19]

But here I see that our Lord descends not only to earth, but even to hell; not as one bound, but as free among the dead; as light that shines in the darkness, "and the darkness did not comprehend it."[20] Wherefore His soul was not left in hell, nor did His holy body on earth see corruption. For Christ "that descended is the same also that ascended … that he might fill all things"[21]; "who went about doing good, and healing all that were oppressed by the devil."[22] And elsewhere we read, He "hath exalted as a giant to run his way … His going forth is from the highest heavens, and his circuit even to the end thereof."[23] Well might St. Paul cry out: "Seek the

---

[18] Psalm 72:25–26
[19] Psalm 22:4
[20] John 1:5
[21] Ephesians 4:10
[22] Acts 10:38
[23] Psalm 18:7

things that are above, where Christ is sitting at the right hand of God."[24] In vain would the Apostle labour to raise our hearts upwards if he did not teach us that the Author of our salvation is sitting in heaven.

But what follows? The matter here is indeed abundant in the extreme; but our limited time does not admit of a lengthened development. By considering Who He is that comes, we see His supreme and ineffable majesty, and by contemplating whence He comes, we behold the great highway clearly laid out to us. The Prophet Isaiah says: "Behold, the name of the Lord cometh from afar."[25] By reflecting whither He comes, we see His inestimable and inconceivable condescension in His descending from highest heavens to abide with us in this miserable prison-house. Who can doubt that there was some grand cause powerful enough to move so sovereign a Majesty to come "from afar," and condescend to enter a place so unworthy of Him as this world of ours. The cause was in truth great. It was His immense mercy, His multiplied compassion, His abundant charity.

For what end must we believe that He came? This question is the next in order to be examined; nor will the search demand much labour, for the end and purpose of His coming is proclaimed by His words and His works. To seek after the one sheep of the hundred that had strayed He hastened from the mountains. For our sake He came down from heaven, that His mercies and His wonders might be openly proclaimed to

---

[24] Colossians 3:1

[25] Isaiah 30:27

the children of men. O' wonderful condescension of God in this search! O' wonderful dignity of man who is thus sought! If he should wish to glory in this dignity, it would not be imputed to him as folly. Not that he need think anything of himself, but let him rejoice that He Who made him should set so high a value on him. For all the riches and glory of the world, all that is desirable therein, is far below this glory—nay, can bear no comparison with it. "Lord, what is man that thou should magnify him? and why settest thou thy heart upon him?"[26]

I still further desire to know why *He* should come to *us*, and not we rather go to Him, for the need was on our side, and it is not usual for the rich to go to the poor, though otherwise willing to assist them. It was indeed our place to go forward to Him, but there stood a twofold impediment in the way; for our eyes were heavy, and He "dwelt in light inaccessible."[27] We lay as paralytics on our beds, and could not raise ourselves to the Divine elevation. Wherefore this most benign Saviour and Physician of souls descended to us from His lofty throne, and tempered His brightness to the weakness of our sight. He clothed Himself with His most glorious and spotless body as with the shade of a lantern, thus attempering to us His splendour. This is that bright and shining cloud upon which the Lord was to descend upon Egypt, as the Prophet Isaiah foretold.[28]

---

[26] Job 7:17
[27] 1 Timothy 1:16
[28] Isaiah 19:1

It is now fitting that we should consider the time of our Lord's coming. He came, as you know, not in the beginning, nor in the midst of time, but in the end of it. This was no unsuitable choice, but a truly wise dispensation of His infinite wisdom, that He might afford help when He saw it was most needed. Truly, "it was evening, and the day was far spent"[29]; the sun of justice had wellnigh set, and but a faint ray of his light and heat remained on earth. The light of Divine knowledge was very small, and as iniquity abounded, the fervour of charity had grown cold. No angel appeared, no prophet spoke. The angelic vision and the prophetic spirit alike had passed away, both hopelessly baffled by the exceeding obduracy and obstinacy of mankind. Then it was that the Son of God said: "Behold, I come."[30] And "while all things were in quiet silence, and the night was in the midst of her course, the almighty word leaped down from heaven from thy royal throne."[31] Of this coming the Apostle speaks: "When the fullness of time was come, God sent his Son."[32] The plenitude and affluence of things temporal had brought on the oblivion and penury of things eternal. Fitly, therefore, did the Eternal God come when things of time were reigning supreme. To pass over other points, such was the temporal peace at the birth of Christ that by the edict of one man the whole world was enrolled.

---

[29] Luke 24:29
[30] Hebrews 10:7
[31] Wisdom of Solomon 18:14, 15
[32] Galatians 4:4

You have now heard Who He is that comes, whence, whither, and to whom He comes; the cause, likewise, and the time of His coming are known to you. One point is yet to be considered—namely, the way by which He came. This must be diligently examined, that we may, as is fitting, go forth to meet Him. As He once came visibly in the body to work our salvation in the midst of the earth, so does He come daily invisibly and in spirit to work the salvation of each individual soul; as it is written: "The Spirit before our face, Christ the Lord." And that we might know this spiritual advent to be hidden, it is said: "Under his shadow we shall live among the Gentiles."[33] Wherefore, if the infirm cannot go far to meet this great Physician, it is at least becoming they should endeavour to raise their heads and lift themselves a little to greet their Saviour. For this, O' man, you are not required to cross the sea, to penetrate the clouds, to scale the mountain-tops. No lofty way is set before you. Turn within thyself to meet thy God, for the Word is nigh in thy mouth and in thy heart. Meet Him by compunction of heart and by confession of mouth, or, at least, go forth from the corruption of a sinful conscience, for it is not becoming that the Author of purity should enter there.

It is delightful to contemplate the manner of His visible coming, for His "ways are beautiful, and all his paths are peace."[34] "Behold," says the Spouse of the Canticles, "he cometh leaping upon the mountains, skipping upon the

---

[33] Lamentations 4:20
[34] Lamentations 4:20

hills."[35] You see Him coming, O' beautiful one, but His previous lying down you could not see, for you said: "Shew me, O' thou whom my soul loveth, where thou feedest, where thou liest."[36] He lay feeding His angels in His endless eternity with the vision of His glorious, unchanging beauty. But know, O' beautiful one, that that vision is become wonderful to thee; it is high, and thou canst not reach it. Nevertheless, behold He hath gone forth from His holy place, and He that had lain feeding His angels hath undertaken to heal us. We shall see Him coming as our food, Whom we were not able to behold while He was feeding His angels in His repose. "Behold, he cometh leaping upon the mountains, skipping upon the hills."[37] The mountains and hills we may consider to be the Patriarchs and the Prophets, and we may see His leaping and skipping in the book of His genealogy. "Abraham begot Isaac, Isaac begot Jacob,"[38] etc. From the mountains came forth the root of Jesse, as you will find from the Prophet Isaiah: "There shall come forth a rod out of the root of Jesse, and a flower shall rise up out of his root, and the Spirit of the Lord shall rest upon him."[39] The same prophet speaks yet more plainly: "Behold, a virgin shall conceive, and bear a Son, and his name shall be called Emmanuel, which is interpreted, 'God with us.' "[40] He Who is first styled a flower is afterwards called Emmanuel, and in the rod is named the virgin. But we must reserve for another day further

---

[35] Canticles 2:8

[36] Canticles 1:6

[37] Song of Solomon 2:8

[38] Matthew 1:2

[39] Isaiah 11:1, 2

[40] Isaiah 7:14

consideration of this sublime mystery, as there is ample material for another sermon, especially as to-day's has been rather long.

## SERMON II

## On the words to Achaz, "Ask Thee a Sign," etc.

"And the Lord spoke again to Achaz, saying: Ask thee a sign of the Lord thy God, either unto the depth of hell, or unto the height above. And Achaz said: I will not ask, and I will not tempt the Lord."[41]

We have heard Isaiah persuading King Achaz to ask for a sign from the Lord, either in the depth of hell, or in the height above. We have heard the King's answer, having the semblance of piety, but not its reality. On this account he deserved to be rejected by Him Who sees the heart, and to Whom the thoughts of men confess. "I will not ask," he says, "and I will not tempt the Lord."[42] Achaz was puffed up with the pomp of the regal throne, and skilled in the cunning words of human wisdom. Isaiah has therefore heard the words: "Go, tell that fox to ask for himself a sign from the Lord unto the depths of hell." For the fox had a hole, but it was in hell, where, if he descended, he would find One Who would catch

---

[41] Isaiah 7:10–12
[42] Isaiah 7:12

the wise in his cunning. Again: "Go," says the Lord, "to that bird, and let him ask for a sign in the heights above," for the bird hath his high nest; but though he ascend to heaven, he will there find Him Who "resisteth the proud," and trampleth with might on the necks of the lofty and high-minded. Achaz refused to ask a sign of that sovereign power, or that incomprehensible depth. Wherefore the Lord Himself promised to the house of David a sign of goodness and charity, that those whom the exhibition of His power could not terrify, nor the manifestations of His wisdom subdue, might be allured by His exceeding love. In the words "depth of hell" may be not unfitly portrayed the charity "greater than which no man hath," that Christ should at death descend even unto hell "for His friends." And in this God would teach Achaz either to dread the majesty of Him Who reigns in the highest, or to embrace the charity of Him Who descends to the lowest. Grievous, therefore, alike to God and man is he who will neither think on majesty with fear nor meditate on charity with love. "Wherefore," the Prophet says, "the Lord himself shall give you a sign."[43]—a sign resplendent alike with majesty and love. "Behold a virgin shall conceive, and bear a Son, and his name shall be called Emmanuel, which is interpreted, 'God with us.' " O' Adam! flee not away, for God is with us! Fear not, O' man, nor be afraid to hear His name; it is "God with us." With us in the likeness of our nature; with us for our service and for our profit. For us He is come as one of us, passible like unto us.

---

[43] Isaiah 7:14

It is said, "He will eat butter and honey"; as if to say, He shall be a little one, fed with infant's food. "That he may know how to reject evil and choose good." As in the case of the forbidden tree, the tree of transgression, so now we hear of an option between good and evil. But the choice of the second Adam is better than that of the first. Choosing the good, He refused the evil; not as He Who loved cursing, and it came upon Him; and He would not have blessing, and it was far from Him.[44] In the prophecy that He would eat butter and honey you may notice the choice of this little one. But may His grace support us, that what He grants us the power to understand He may likewise enable us to explain!

From milk we obtain two substances, butter and cheese. Butter is oily and moist; cheese, on the contrary, is hard. Our little one knew well how to choose when, eating the butter, He did not taste the cheese. Behold, therefore, how He chose the best; He assumed our nature free from all corruption of sin. Of sinners we read that their heart is curdled as milk; the purity of their nature is corrupted by the fermentation of malice and iniquity.

And now let us turn to the honey. Our bee feeds among lilies, and dwells in the flowery country of the angels. This bee flew to the city of Nazareth, which is, interpreted, a flower; He came to the sweet-smelling flower of perpetual virginity; He settled upon it, He clove to it. But bees, besides their sweet honey, have likewise their sharp sting. The Prophet that sang of the mercy and judgment of the Lord,

---

[44] Psalm 108:18

knew that this bee had a sting as well as honey.[45] Nevertheless, when He descended to us He brought honey only—that is, mercy, not judgment—so that to the disciples who wished to call down fire from heaven on the cities that would not receive Him, He answered: "The Son of Man is not come to judge the world, but to save it."[46] Our bee had no sting in His mortal life; amid the extremity of insult He showed mercy, not judgment. Christ, then, may be symbolized both as a bee and as the flower springing from the rod. And, as we know, the rod is the Virgin Mother of God.

This flower, the Son of the Virgin, is "white and ruddy, chosen out of thousands."[47] It is the flower on which the angels desire to look, the flower whose perfume shall revive the dead, the flower, as He Himself declares, of the field, not of the garden. This flower grew and flourished in the field independent of all human culture; unsown by the hand of man, unfilled by the spade, or fattened by moisture. So did the womb of Mary blossom. As a rich pasture it brought forth the flower of eternal beauty, whose freshness shall never fade nor see corruption, whose glory is to everlasting. O' sublime virgin rod, that raisest thy holy head aloft, even to Him Who sitteth on the throne, even to the Lord of Majesty! And this is not wonderful, for thou hast planted thy roots deeply in the soil of humility. O' truly celestial plant, than which none more precious, none more holy! O' true tree of life, alone deemed worthy to bear the fruit of salvation! Thou art caught,

---

[45] Psalm 100:1
[46] John 12:47
[47] Canticles 5:10

O' wicked serpent, caught in thy own cunning; thy falsity is laid bare. Two evils thou hadst imputed to thy Creator; thou hadst defamed Him by envy and by lying, but in both imputations thou art convicted a liar. He to whom thou hadst promised that he should not die did die, "and the truth of the Lord remaineth for ever."[48] And now answer, if thou canst, what tree God could forbid man, seeing He denied him not this chosen rod, this sublime fruit? For "he that spared not his own Son, how hath he not with him given us all things?"[49]

It is now surely clear how the Virgin is the royal way by which the Saviour has drawn near to us, coming forth from her womb as a Bridegroom from His bridal chamber. Holding on, therefore, to this way, let us endeavour to ascend to Him by her, through Whom He descended to us; let us seek His grace through her by whom He came to succour our need.

O' blessed finder of grace! Mother of life! Mother of salvation! may we through thee have access to thy Son, that through thee we may be received by Him Who through thee was given to us. May thy integrity and purity excuse before Him the stain of our corruption; may thy humility, so pleasing to God, obtain from Him the pardon of our vanity. May thy abundant charity cover the multitude of our iniquity, and thy glorious fruitfulness supply our indigence of merits. Our Lady, our Mediatrix, our Advocate, reconcile us to thy Son, commend us to thy Son, present us to thy Son. By the grace thou hast found, by the prerogative thou didst merit, by the

---

[48] Psalm 116:2
[49] Romans 8:32

mercy thou didst bring forth, obtain, O' blessed one, that He Who vouchsafed to become partaker of our infirmity and misery, may, through thy intercession, make us partakers of His blessedness and glory, Jesus Christ, thy Son, our Lord, Who is God blessed above all for evermore. Amen.

# II

# ON THE "MISSUS EST"

## *On The "Missus EST"*



*The holy Abbot St. Bernard's Preface to His "Praises of the Virgin Mother."*—I am in straits. My devotion bids me write; my occupations hinder me. Nevertheless, as sickness prevents me at present from following the community exercises with my brethren, I will not spend uselessly that little leisure which I contrive to find by shortening my night's rest. Besides, it is a pleasure to me to attempt what has been for so long in my mind—namely, to speak or write something to the praise of the Virgin Mother, upon that portion of St. Luke's Gospel which contains the history of the Annunciation of our Lord's birth.

"And while I devote myself to this work, so long as the brethren over whom I am placed, and whom it is my happy duty to serve, do not find me less ready to minister either to their pressing needs, or even to their reasonable demands upon my time, I think none ought to object to my thus satisfying my devotion.

## HOMILY I

### Praises of the Virgin-Mother

"The angel Gabriel was sent from God to a city of Galilee called Nazareth, to a virgin espoused to a man whose name was Joseph, of the house of David; and the virgin's name was Mary."[50]

What can be the Evangelist's intention in mentioning in this text so many proper names? I think it is that he would not have us listen carelessly to what he has been at such pains to relate. He names the messenger sent, the Lord by Whom, the Virgin *to* whom he is sent, the spouse of the Virgin, with the race of each; their city, too, and country are pointed out by name. And why all this explanation? Can the Evangelist have said anything superfluous? By no means. If not a leaf from a tree, nor a single sparrow falls to the ground without a cause and the knowledge of our heavenly Father, can I suppose that one superfluous word would fall from the lips of the holy Evangelist, especially when he is giving the history of the Word Incarnate? Certainly I cannot. Full is every word of divinest mystery, redolent of sweetest heavenly perfume; to him, that is, who searches it diligently and knows how to draw "honey from the rock and oil from the flinty stone."[51] For in that day "the mountains dropped down with sweetness, and the hills flowed with milk"[52] and honey. When the heavens dropped down dew and the clouds rained the Just One, then the joyous earth was opened and budded forth a Saviour, then the Lord gave goodness and our earth yielded forth her fruit.[53] On that mountain of mountains heaped up

---

[50] Luke 1:26, 27
[51] Deuteronomy 32:13
[52] Joel 3:18
[53] Psalm 84:13

and fat "mercy and truth met each other, justice and peace kissed."[54] In that day, too, one mountain was especially blessed among mountains—namely, the Evangelist himself, when, with mellifluous eloquence, he made known to us the beginning of our long-desired salvation, like some delightful south wind bringing delicious spiritual perfumes caught from the rising Sun of justice. Would that God would now also "send forth his words" and "let them flow to us"; may "his Spirit breathe," may the Evangelist's words be intelligible to us; may they become to our hearts "more desirable than gold and precious stones"; may they be sweeter to us than honey and the honeycomb.

"The angel Gabriel was sent from God."[55] I do not think that this was one of the lower angels who for one cause or another are often sent to earth; and I gather it from his name, which is interpreted "Strength of God"; because, also, he was not sent as is usual from a superior spirit, but from God Himself. For this reason it is said "sent from God," or appointed by God, lest we should suppose that God had revealed His design to anyone before the Blessed Virgin. Among the blessed spirits themselves Gabriel alone was excepted, for he alone was found worthy of his name and embassy. The name befits the messenger, for could Christ, the Power of God, be more fittingly announced than by him who bore a similar name? Nor is it unbecoming or unsuitable that the Lord and His nuncio should bear the same title, for though the name is alike, the cause for which it is given differs.

<hr>

[54] Psalm 84:13
[55] Luke 1:26

Christ is called the Strength or Power of God in quite another sense than the angel. In the angel it is merely an appellation; in Christ it expresses a substantial quality. Christ is called, and *is*, the Power of God. Stronger than the strong-armed, the Prince of this world, who kept his goods in peace, He came down upon him, waged war against him, and with His own arm bore away the spoils. The angel is called the Strength of God either because he had merited the prerogative of officially announcing the Advent of the Power of God, or in order that he might strengthen and support the Virgin, by nature timid and bashful, whom the novelty of the miracle might terrify and overpower. This he did when he said: "Fear not, Mary, thou hast found grace with God."[56] It is not unreasonable to suppose, though the Evangelist does not mention the angel's name, that this was the same archangel who strengthened and comforted Mary's spouse, a humble and timorous man. "Fear not, Joseph," he says, "son of David, to take unto thee Mary thy wife."[57] Gabriel, therefore, was most fitly chosen for this work, or rather the name was imposed because of the embassy.

The angel, therefore, is sent from God. Whither? "To a city of Galilee called Nazareth." Let us see if, as Nathaniel says, anything good can come from Nazareth. *Nazareth* is interpreted *flower*. The seed of this flower seems to me to have been cast from heaven upon the earth by the heavenly words spoken and the promises made to our fathers Abraham, Isaac, and Jacob. Of this seed it is written, "Except the Lord of Hosts

---

[56] Luke 1:30
[57] Matthew 1:20

had left us seed, we had been as Sodom, and we should have been as Gomorrha."[58] This seed flowered in the wonders displayed in the going forth from Egypt; it flowered in the signs and figures that marked the journey of the Israelites through the wilderness to the Promised Land; it flowered in the vision sand prophetical declarations of the Prophets, in the establishment and order of the kingdom and priesthood before the coming of Christ. But Christ is rightly understood to be the fruit of this seed and flower. For David says, "The Lord will give goodness, the earth shall yield her fruit."[59] And again: "Of the fruit of thy womb, I will set one upon thy throne."[60] In Nazareth, therefore, Christ's future birth is announced, because when the flower has budded we have hope that fruit will follow. But, as in the formation of the fruit the flower decays and drops off, so with the appearance of the Truth in the flesh, the figures passed away.

As the Apostle says, "These things happened to them in figure."[61] Hence Nazareth is called a city of Galilee—that is, change, or passage. We who have the fruit see that these flowers have passed away, and that even while they seemed to flourish their future decay was foretold. For David says: "In the morning he shall grow up like grass: in the morning he shall flourish and pass away, in the evening he shall fall, grow dry and wither."[62] In the evening—that is, in the fullness of time, when "God sent his only Son made of a woman, made

---

[58] Isaiah 1:9
[59] Psalm 84:13
[60] Psalm 131:11
[61] 1 Corinthians 10:6
[62] Psalm 89:6

under the law."[63] "Behold," He says, "I make all things new." Hence it is again written, "The grass is withered and the flower is fallen: but the word of the Lord remaineth for ever."[64] I think there is no doubt that the Word is Christ, and Christ is the good fruit that remaineth for ever. But where is the grass that withered? where the flower that fell off? Let the Prophet answer: "All flesh is grass, and all the glory thereof as the flower of the field."[65] If all flesh is grass, the carnal Jews were grass; and did not the grass wither when that people, devoid of spiritual unction, adhered to the dry letter? And did not the flower fall off when they no longer gloried in the law? If the flower did not fall, where is their kingdom, their priesthood, their prophets, their temple? Where are those wonders in which they were wont to glory and to say: "How great things have we heard and known, and our fathers have told us"[66]? And again: "How great things he commanded our fathers, that they should make known to their children."[67]

"To Nazareth, a city of Galilee." To this city the angel Gabriel was sent from God. To whom? To a Virgin espoused to a man whose name was Joseph." Who is this Virgin so reverently saluted by the angel? and so lowly as to be espoused to a carpenter? Beautiful commingling of virginity with humility! That soul is in no small degree pleasing to God, in Whom humility commends virginity, and virginity adorns humility. But how much more worthy of veneration is she, in

---

[63] Galatians 4:4

[64] Isaiah 40:7, 8

[65] Isaiah 40:6

[66] Psalm 77:3

[67] Psalm 77:3

whom fecundity exalts humility, and child-bearing consecrates virginity. Virginity is a commendable virtue, but humility an indispensable one. The first is of counsel, the latter of precept. Of the one it is said, "He that can take, let him take it."[68] Of the other, "Unless you become as little children, you shall not enter into the kingdom of heaven."[69] To the one reward is offered; the other is exacted under a threat. Again, we can be saved without virginity, not without humility. A soul that has to deplore the loss of virginity may still be acceptable to God by humility: without humility, I will venture to say that even the virginity of Mary would not have been pleasing to Him, the Divine Majesty. Upon whom shall my spirit rest, if not on him that is humble and peaceable?[70] He says not on the virgin, but on the humble. If, therefore, Mary had not been humble the Spirit would not have rested on her. If the Holy Spirit had not rested on her, she would never have become fruitful; for how without Him could she have conceived of Him? Therefore, as she herself testifies, in order that she might conceive of the Holy Ghost, God the Father "regarded the humility of his handmaid,"[71] rather than her virginity. And if by her virginity she was acceptable to Him, nevertheless, it was by her humility that she conceived Him. Hence it is evident that it was her humility that rendered even her virginity pleasing to God.

---

[68] Matthew 19:12

[69] Matthew 18:3

[70] Isaiah 40:2

[71] Luke 1:48

A proud virgin, what can you say? Mary forgets herself and her virginity, and glories only in her humility, and you, neglecting humility, presume to pride yourself on your virginity. She says: "He hath had regard to the humility of his handmaid." And who is this handmaid? A holy virgin, a prudent virgin, a devout virgin. Are you more chaste than she? Are you more devout? Is your purity more pleasing than the chastity of Mary, that without humility, you deem it sufficient for you, when without humility her virginity could not find favour? The more honourable the gift of chastity, the greater the injury you do it in tarnishing its beauty within you by any admixture of pride. It would have been better for you not to be a virgin than to be puffed up and grow insolent by virginity. Virginity is not for all; it is for the few; and there are few among the few that unite humility with virginity. Wherefore, if you can only admire the virginity of Mary without being able to imitate it, study to copy her humility, and it will be sufficient for you. But if with virginity you possess humility, then you are great indeed.

But in Mary there is something more wonderful still: it is the union of fecundity with virginity. Since the beginning of the world it had not been heard that a woman was at once a virgin and a mother. And if you consider of whom she is the mother, how great will be your admiration of her exalted dignity! Do you feel as if you can never sufficiently praise it? Do you not judge, and rightly, that she who has the God-man for her Son is exalted in greatness above all the choirs of angels? Did not Mary confidently call the God and Lord of

Angels her Son, saying: "Son, why hast thou done so to us?"[72] Which of the angels would have presumed thus to speak? It is sufficient for them and something great, that while by nature they are spirits by grace they are made and called angels, as David says: "Who maketh his angels spirits."[73] In confidently calling God her Son, Mary acknowledges herself mother of that Majesty Whom those angels serve with reverential awe. Neither does God disdain to be called what He vouchsafed to be. For the Evangelist adds shortly after, "And he was subject to them."[74] Who was subject? God, to man. God to Whom the angels are subject. God, Whom the powers and principalities obey, was subject to Mary. And not only to Mary, but to Joseph also for Mary's sake. Consider, then, and choose which you will most admire, the gracious condescension of the Son, or the surpassing dignity of the mother. Both are amazing; both are miraculous. That a God should obey a woman is humility without example; that a woman should command the Son of God is a dignity without parallel. In the praise of virgins we hear that wonderful verse: "They shall follow the Lamb whithersoever he goeth."[75] But what praise, think you, is worthy of her who leads the way before Him? Learn, O' man, to obey; learn, O' earth, to be subject; learn, O' dust, to be submissive. The Evangelist, speaking of your Creator, says: "He was subject to them"—that is, of course, to Mary and Joseph.

---

[72] Luke 2:48

[73] Psalm 103:4; Hebrews 1:7

[74] Luke 2:51

[75] Revelation 14:4

Blush, O' dust and ashes, and be ashamed to be proud. God humbles Himself, and do you exalt yourself? God submits to man, and do you desire to domineer over your fellow-man? In so doing you prefer yourself to your Creator. Would that when such thoughts assail me, God would vouchsafe to make me the same reproach as to His Apostle: "Get behind me, Satan, for thou savourest not the things that are of God."[76] As often as I seek distinction among men, so often do I dispute the pre-eminence with my God, and then assuredly I savour not the things that are of God, since of Him it is said: "He was subject to them." If, O' man, you disdain to imitate the example of your fellow-man, you cannot find it degrading to follow that of your Maker. If you cannot follow Him "whithersoever he goeth," at least follow Him in the most safe road of humility, for, from this straight path should even virgins deviate they will not "follow the Lamb whithersoever he goeth." The Lamb is followed by the innocent soul and by the once sin stained but now humble and repentant soul; by the proud virgin, likewise, He is followed, but assuredly not "whithersoever he goeth." The penitent cannot rise to the purity of the Lamb without spot, the proud soul cannot descend to the meekness of Him Who, not before His shearers only, but even before His executioners, was dumb and opened not his mouth. It is safer for the sinner to follow in humility than to be proud in virginity, because the sinner by his humility makes satisfaction for, and purges away his

<hr>

[76] Matthew 16:23

impurity, whereas, the purity of the other is polluted by pride.

Happy was Mary in whom neither humility nor virginity was wanting. O' glorious virginity! which fecundity honoured, but did not contaminate. O' singular humility! that a fruitful virginity elevated but did not destroy. O' incomparable fecundity! in which virginity was associated with humility. Which of them is not wonderful, incomparable, unique? In pondering them, we are at a loss to decide which is the more worthy of admiration: the Virgin's fecundity, the Mother's integrity, or the adorable dignity of her offspring; or, again, that in such sublime elevation she still preserves her humility. Can we be surprised that God, Who is wonderful in His saints, should also show Himself wonderful in His Mother? Admire, ye married, and reverence her integrity in corruptible flesh! Ye sacred virgins, behold with astonishment this fruitful virgin! Let all Christians imitate the humility of the Mother of God! O' holy angels, honour the Mother of your King! He is at once our King and yours, the Redeemer of our race, the replenisher of your city. To Him Who with you is so glorious, with us so humble, be rendered for ages without end, both by us and by you, the reverence due to His dignity and the honour and glory worthy of His infinite condescension. Amen. Amen.

# HOMILY II

## The Mission of the Angel

No one, surely, will doubt that in the kingdom of God the Queen of virgins will join—nay, rather, will take the lead—in the canticle which only virgins sing. Further than this, I think she will gladden the City of God with a yet sweeter and more thrilling melody, whose enrapturing strains not one among the virgins will be worthy to utter. This song will be reserved to her who alone could glory in her child-bearing—a Divine child-bearing. In thus glorying, she glories not in herself, but in Him Whom she brought forth; for God would certainly enrich with singular glory in heaven that Mother whom He prevented with the surpassing grace of bringing Him into the world without prejudice to her virginity. Such a birth was becoming a God Who alone could be born of a virgin. Such a child-bearing was befitting one who had a God for her Child. Therefore, it was needful that the Creator of man, in order to unite Himself to the human race, should choose—nay, create—a Mother whom He knew to be worthy of, and acceptable to, Himself. He willed her to be an immaculate virgin, that she might merit to have for her Son the Spotless One, Who was about to take away the sins of the world. He willed her, too, to be humble, from whom He Who was meek and humble should come into the world, He Who was to show to all men a salutary example of these two virtues. He gave fruitfulness to the Virgin whom He had previously inspired with the desire of vowing her virginity to God, and whom He had also enriched with the grace of humility. Otherwise, how could the angel have proclaimed her "full of grace" if she had possessed any of the least good that was not the effect of Divine grace? In order, therefore, that she who was to conceive and bring forth the Holy of Holies might be holy in body, she received the gift of virginity, and that she might be holy in mind, she received the gift of humility. With these gems of virtue the royal Virgin was adorned, and, radiant with the double splendour of holiness in body and mind, she was no sooner revealed to the heavenly citizens than they fixed upon her their admiring gaze. The King Himself stooped to desire her beauty, and sent her His heavenly ambassador. And this is what the Evangelist makes known when he says that the angel was sent from God to the Virgin. From God to the Virgin—that is, from the highest to the lowliest; from the Lord to His handmaid; from the Creator to His creature. How great the condescension of God! How pre-eminent the excellence of the Virgin!

Hasten, O' ye mothers! Press forward, ye daughters of Eve! Come quickly, all you who, on account of Eve's fall, bring forth in sorrow! Approach the Virgin's chamber; enter, if you can, the modest room of your Sister; for, behold! God sends a message to the Virgin. An angel addresses Mary. Place your ear close to the wall; listen to what he announces; perchance you may receive a word of consolation. Rejoice, O' father Adam, and exult yet more, O' mother Eve—you who, though the parents of all, were their destroyers even before you became their parents. Be consoled now in your daughter, and in such a daughter! you especially, O' Eve, from whom the evil first originated, and whose reproach passed as a disgraceful legacy to womanhood. The time is at hand when that reproach shall be taken away. Wherefore, O' Eve, hasten to Mary; hasten, O' Mother, to your daughter. Let the daughter answer for the mother; let her take away her mother's reproach; let her satisfy also for her father Adam, for if he fell by a woman, behold, he is now raised up by a woman. God gave a woman in exchange for a woman; a prudent woman for one that was foolish; a humble woman for one who was proud; one who, instead of the fruit of death, shall give you to eat of the tree of life, and who, in place of the poisoned food of bitterness, will bring forth the fruit of everlasting sweetness. Change now, O' Adam, your wicked words of excuse to the song of endless thanksgiving, and say: "O Lord, the woman whom thou hast given me, gave me of the tree of life; and I have eaten, and its fruit has been sweeter than honey to my mouth, and by it thou hast given me life." This is why the angel was sent to the Virgin. O' wondrous and most honourable Virgin! O' woman singularly venerable! admirable among all women! thou who hast satisfied for thy parents, and restored life to their posterity.

"The Angel was sent to a virgin." A virgin in body, a virgin in mind, a virgin by profession, a virgin such as the Apostle describes "holy in body and in mind."[77] She is no recent and chance discovery, but the object of God's eternal predilection; foreknown by the Most High, prepared for Himself, guarded by angels, pointed out by the Patriarchs, promised by the Prophets. Search the Scriptures, and prove

--------

[77] 1 Corinthians 7:34

the truth of my words. To give a few testimonies out of many, of what other woman could God have spoken when He said to the serpent, "I will place enmities between thee and the woman?"[78] And if you still doubt whether Mary were that woman, listen to what follows: "She shall crush thy head."[79] To whom but to Mary was such a victory reserved? Undoubtedly the empoisoned head of the serpent was crushed by Mary, who brought to naught every suggestion of the Evil One, as well as regards carnal allurements as intellectual pride. Again, what other woman did Solomon seek? The Wise Man knew the frailty of that sex, the weakness of their bodies, the inconstancy of their minds. But he had read God's promise, and saw that it was fitting that the enemy who had been victorious over the human race by means of a woman should by another woman be himself overcome. Wondering exceedingly, he exclaimed: "Who shall find a valiant woman?"[80] As if to say, if upon a woman depends alike the salvation of our race, its restoration to innocence, and its victory over our common enemy, she must indeed be valiant to be fitted for so sublime an undertaking. But "who shall find a valiant woman?" And lest he should be accused of asking in despondency, he adds in prophecy, "The price of her is as of things brought from afar off, and from the remotest coasts." Such a price is not small, nor mean, nor of light account, nor is it from earth, but from heaven. And not even from the heaven nearest the earth, but from the highest heavens—"His

---

[78] Genesis 3:15
[79] Genesis 3:15
[80] Proverbs 31:10

going forth is from the height of heaven."[81] And what, again, was that bush shown to Moses, burning and yet unburnt, but Mary who brought forth without sorrow? In Aaron's rod, which flowered without moisture, she is also typified, for she conceived without knowing man.

The mystery of this stupendous miracle Isaiah more clearly points out when he says: "There shall come forth a rod out of the root of Jesse, and a flower shall rise up out of his root." The rod is the Virgin, the flower the Virgin's Child. There is nothing unfitting in Christ being represented under different figures for different causes. So we may speak of Him as the rod, an emblem of power, or as the flower, emblem of fragrance, or as the fruit, that of sweetness; whilst by the leaves we may understand His ceaseless protection—that protection which He continually extends over the little ones who take refuge under His shadow from the heat of earthly desires, and from the face of them that afflict them. O' good and desirable shade, under the protection of Jesus, where he that is pursued finds refuge, and where the weary obtain rest and refreshment! Have mercy on me, O' Jesus, for my soul confides in Thee, and under the shadow of Thy wings I will hope till iniquity pass by.

Other references might be quoted equally suitable to the Virgin Mother and to the Son of God—Gideon's fleece, for instance, cut from the flesh without wounding it, and placed on the dry ground, where the dry fleeces are in turn

---

[81] Psalm 18:7

moistened by the dew. This similitude represents the flesh assumed from the flesh of Mary without injury to her virginity. Upon *it* Heaven dropped down dew, filling it with the plenitude of the Divinity, and from that fullness we have all received—we who, but for it, were as parched and arid soil. The Psalmist seems to refer very beautifully to this fact in Gideon's history. In Ps. 71 we read: "He shall descend like rain upon the fleece, and as showers falling gently upon the earth."[82] Gently at first, and without noise of human operation, He fell softly into the Virgin's womb; afterwards, when the Apostles announced Him, it was with the noise of words and the display of miracles. For they were mindful of the words spoken to them when they were sent: "What I tell you in the dark, speak ye in the light, and what you hear in the ear, preach ye on the housetops."[83] This injunction they carried out, for "their sound has gone forth to the whole earth, and their words to the uttermost ends of the world."[84]

Let us now give ear to Jeremias, who foretells a new and unheard-of wonder, while he ardently desires, and confidently promises, the coming of Him Whose presence he might not behold. "God has created a new thing on the earth, a woman shall encompass a man."[85] Who is this woman, and who is this man? And if a man, how is He encompassed by a woman? "Can a man," said Nicodemus, "return to his mother's womb, and be born again?"[86] I turn for my answer

---

[82] Psalm 71:6
[83] Matthew 10:27
[84] Psalm 18:5; Romans 10:18
[85] Jeremiah 31:22
[86] John 3:4

to the Virgin's conception and child-bearing, yet even there, among the many new and wonderful mysteries that meet the consideration of the diligent inquirer, this which the Prophet here proposes will excite admiration. *There* is seen length abbreviated, width straightened, height, lowered, depth filled up. There we behold light withholding its rays, the Word an infant, the Living Water athirst, Him Who is the Bread of Heaven suffering hunger. Attend and see how Omnipotence is ruled, Wisdom instructed, Power sustained; the God Who rejoices the angels is become a Babe at the breast; He Who consoles the afflicted lies weeping in a manger. Attend and see how joy is made sorrowful, strength becomes weakness, life death; but—what is equally wonderful—*that* sorrow gives joy, that weakness imparts strength, that death restores life.

Who does not now see that I have found what I sought, and that we behold "a woman encompassing a man" when we see Mary enclosing in her womb Jesus, the Man-God? For I may call Jesus a man not only when He was proclaimed "a prophet mighty in work and word," but also when His tender infant limbs lay in the womb of His Mother, or gently nestled on her bosom. Jesus, then, was a man even before His birth; not in age, but in wisdom; not in strength of body, but in vigour of mind; not by the development of His members, but by the perfection of His intelligence: for the wisdom of Jesus was as great at His conception as at His birth, when He was a child as when He was a perfect man. Whether hidden in the womb or weeping in the manger, whether a boy among the doctors or teaching the people in perfect manhood, He was ever equally full of the Holy Ghost. There was no moment of His human life when that plenitude of the Holy Spirit which He received at His conception suffered either diminution or augmentation. From the first He was perfect, from the first He was full of "the spirit of wisdom and understanding, of the spirit of counsel and fortitude, of the spirit of knowledge and piety, and of the spirit of the fear of the Lord."[87] Yet be not surprised if you read elsewhere: "And Jesus advanced in wisdom and age, and grace before God and men."[88] What is here said of wisdom and grace must be understood not of their essence, but of their outward appearance. That is to say, that our Lord never acquired what He did not before possess; but that He seemed to acquire it when He willed it to appear.

You, O' Christian soul, advance not when and as you would; you find your progress apparently checked, your life at the disposal of another. But the Child Jesus Who guides your life regulated also His own. When He would, and on what occasions He would, He appeared wise; when and as He willed, more wise; and as He willed, most wise; though all the while He never was aught but sublimest wisdom. In like manner, though He was ever full of all the grace which it was fitting He should have before God and men, according as He judged proper, He showed now more, now less, according to the merits of the observers, or as He knew their spiritual needs required it. It is evident, therefore, that if in bodily

---

[87] Isaiah 11:2, 3
[88] Luke 2:52

development Jesus did not always appear a man, His mind was ever fully developed.

But let us see if Isaiah, who above explained the new flowers on Aaron's rod, has not also brought light to bear on this "new thing" of Jeremias. He says: "Behold, a virgin shall conceive, and bring forth a son."[89] Here for the "woman" we have "virgin." What does He say of the "man"? "And his name shall be called Emmanuel, that is, 'God with us.' " Therefore the woman encompassing a man is the Virgin conceiving the Son of God. How stupendous this very miracle wrought in a virgin and from a virgin's nature—a miracle which so many other miracles had foreshadowed, so many oracles proclaimed. The spirit of the Prophets was ever the same. Though at different times and in different ways, it was not in a different spirit that they foresaw and predicted the same truth. What is shown by Moses' burning bush, by Aaron's flowering rod, by Gideon's dew and fleece, is clearly spoken of by Solomon in the valiant woman and her price; more clearly by Jeremias in the woman and the man; most plainly by Isaiah in the Virgin and Emmanuel. To Gabriel it was reserved to point her out by his salutation. For of her the Evangelist says: "The angel Gabriel was sent from God to a virgin espoused to Joseph."[90]

"To a virgin espoused." Why espoused? In order that Joseph, by carefully studying her life and conversation, might be a most faithful witness to her purity, for it was intolerable

---

[89] Isaiah 7:14
[90] Luke 1:27

that any slur should be cast on the Mother of God. But could not God have given some sign which would have preserved His own birth from infamy, and His Mother's honour from suspicion? Undoubtedly He could, but not without discovering to the devil what He had revealed to men; and it was necessary that this secret of God's counsel should for a time be concealed from the prince of this world. Not that God had any obstacle to fear from the devil, had He chosen to make His operation manifest, but because He acts not only powerfully, but wisely, in all that He does, and preserves an exquisite order in all His works, observing the fitting times and circumstances for their performance. Therefore, in this glorious work of our redemption. He likewise wished to show forth His wisdom as well as His power. He could have accomplished it by other means, but He willed to reconcile man to Himself by the same means and in the same order as He knew man had fallen. As the devil had first deceived the woman, then overcome the man by the woman, so he was to be deceived by a woman, a virgin, and afterwards be openly attacked and conquered by the Man (Christ). Thus, by a device of infinite compassion, God laid bare the fraud of malice. The power of Christ broke the strength of the Evil One, and the might and wisdom of God confounded the devil's malice and craft.

It was necessary, then, that Mary should be espoused to Joseph, in order that what was holy might be concealed from the unholy, that the virginity of Mary might be proved to her spouse, and that the Virgin might be preserved from suspicion and her reputation protected. What more wise? What more worthy of Divine Providence?

But it is written: "Joseph, her husband, being a just man, and not willing publicly to expose her, had a mind to put her away privately."[91] Truly, because he was just, he would not expose her publicly; for as he would not have been just had he countenanced one that was guilty, neither would he have been just if he had condemned one whose innocence he had proved. Since, then, he was just and unwilling to expose her, why had he a mind to put her away? I give you on this point not my own opinion, but that of the Fathers. Joseph's reason was the same as Peter's when he said, "Depart from me, for I am a sinful man, O' Lord," and that of the centurion when he exclaimed, "I am not worthy that thou shouldst enter under my roof." Joseph looked on himself as a sinner and as unworthy to entertain one in whom he beheld a superhuman dignity. He beheld with awe in the Virgin-Mother a certain sign of the Divine Presence, and as he could not penetrate the mystery, he wished to put her away. Peter was struck with awe at the greatness of Christ's power; the centurion by the majesty of His presence; and Joseph was naturally afraid at the novelty and splendour of the miracle and the depth of the mystery. We need not wonder that he thought himself unworthy of the society of such a virgin when we hear the holy Elizabeth exclaim with fear and trembling: "Whence is this to me that the mother of my Lord should come to me?"[92] But if, on the other hand, any believe that Joseph suspected

---

[91] Matthew 1:19
[92] Luke 1:43

Mary, this very doubt of his was necessary, and merited to be dispelled by Divine intervention; for it is written: "But while he thought on these things" (that is, the putting her away privately), "behold, an angel of the Lord appeared to him in his sleep, saying: Joseph, son of David, fear not to take unto thee Mary, thy wife, for that which is conceived in her is of the Holy Ghost."[93] For the above reasons, therefore, Mary was espoused to Joseph.

What are we to think of the dignity of Joseph, who deserved to be called and to be regarded as the father of our Saviour? We may draw a parallel between him and the great Patriarch. As the first Joseph was by the envy of his brothers sold and sent into Egypt, the second Joseph fled into Egypt with Christ to escape the envy of Herod. The chaste Patriarch remained faithful to his master, despite the evil suggestions of his mistress. St. Joseph, recognizing in his wife the Virgin Mother of his Lord, guarded her with the utmost fidelity and chastity. To the Joseph of old was given interpretation of dreams, to the new Joseph a share in heavenly secrets. His predecessor kept a store of corn, not for himself, but for the whole nation; *our* Joseph received the Living Bread from heaven, that he might preserve it for his own salvation and that of all the world. A good and faithful servant was the Joseph to whom Mary, the Mother of the Saviour, was espoused; a faithful and prudent servant whom our Lord chose for the comfort of His Mother and the nurse of His own

---

[93] Matthew 1:20

childhood, as well as the only and most trustworthy co-operator in the Divine design.

We read in this place that he was of the house of David. Yea, truly was this our Joseph descended from royal stock, a man of noble race and yet nobler mind, the son of David, in nothing degenerating from the nobility of David, his father. He was son of David less by kinship of blood than by inheritance of faith, of devotion, and of holiness of life—a man whom, like another David, God found according to His own heart, and to whom He entrusted His most precious secret; to whom, as to David, He made manifest the uncertain and hidden things of his wisdom, and to whom He revealed a mystery hidden from the great ones of the world. To Joseph it was given to behold Him Whom many kings and prophets had desired to see and had not seen, to hear and had not heard. And not only was he allowed to behold Him and listen to His words, but he might bear Jesus in his arms, guide His steps, embrace and caress Him, feed and protect Him.

It is also supposed that Mary was of the same house of David, otherwise she would not have been espoused to a man of that house. Both, then, were of the royal race; but in Mary was fulfilled the truth which the Lord swore unto David; in Joseph we have the witness of its fulfilment. The verse concludes with the words: "And the virgin's name was Mary."[94]

---

[94] Luke 1:27

We will dwell a while on this name, which is, rightly interpreted, "Star of the Sea," and is therefore admirably appropriate to the Virgin Mother. Fitly is she compared to a star, which, in giving forth its light, suffers no waning, since she brought forth her Son without stain to her virginity. As the ray of the star lessens not its brightness, so the Son of Mary detracted in no way from her integrity. She is therefore that glorious star which arose from Jacob, and which cast its radiance over the whole world—the star whose splendour rejoices heaven, terrifies hell, and sheds its mild and beneficent influence on the poor exiles of earth. She is truly the Star which, being placed over this world's tempestuous sea, shines forth by the lustre of her merits and example.

O' you who find yourself tossed about by the storms of life, turn not your eyes from the brightness of this Star, if you would not be overwhelmed by its boisterous waves. If the winds of temptations rise, if you fall among the rocks of tribulations, look up at the Star, call on Mary. If anger, covetousness, or other passions beat on the vessel of your soul, look up to Mary. If you begin to sink in the gulf of melancholy and despair, think on Mary. In dangers, in distress, in perplexities, think on Mary, call on Mary. Let her not depart from your lips, let her not depart from your heart, and, that you may win the suffrage of her prayers, never depart from the example of her life. Following her, you will never go astray; when you implore her aid, you will never yield to despair; thinking on her, you will not err; under her patronage you will never wander; beneath her protection you will not fear; she being your guide, you will not weary; if she be your propitious Star, you will arrive safely in the port, and experience for yourself the truth of the words, "And the virgin's name was Mary."

And let us not turn too rapidly from the brightness of this transcendent luminary, for, in the words of the Apostle, "It is good for us to be here." Let us, then, gaze in silent contemplation on that which words are powerless to explain. Thus shall we repair our spiritual powers, and be enabled to consider more fervently the points that follow.


## HOMILY III

### Colloquy of the Blessed Virgin and the Angel

"Woe is me," says the Prophet, "because I have held my peace, because I am a man of unclean lips."[95] I, too, will say "Woe is me," not because I have held my peace, but because I have spoken, for I, too, "am a man of unclean lips." How many vain, erroneous, and unbecoming words hath not this my vile mouth uttered, which now presumes to speak of the things of heaven! Would that there were brought to me from the altar above, not one "live coal" only, but a great ball of fire to touch and cleanse my unworthy lips, and make me fit to repeat the chaste and beautiful colloquies between the angel and the Virgin. The Evangelist says:

---

[95] Isaiah 6:5

"And the angel being come in to her" (that is, to Mary), "said, Hail, full of grace, the Lord is with thee."[96] Where did he come in to her? I think into the secrecy of her virginal chamber, where perchance, having closed the door upon her, Mary was praying to her Father in secret. And it was not difficult for the angel to penetrate through the closed door into the inner chamber of the Virgin. Neither bolts nor bars could oppose the subtlety of his nature, to which all solid substances yield, and which bears him whither the impetus of his spirit leads him. We cannot suppose that he found *her* door unclosed, who so studiously avoided the company and conversation of men, lest her recollection should be disturbed or her virtue threatened. Closed, therefore, at that hour was the dwelling of that most prudent Virgin, but to men, not to angels. For the angels are wont to be near those who pray; they delight in beholding them raise their pure hands to heaven; and with glad service they present to God the sacrifices of devotion which they offer in the odour of sweetness. How pleasing to the Most High were the prayers of Mary is well shown by the reverence with which the angel saluted her.

Being come into her, he said: "Hail, full of grace, the Lord is with thee." In the Acts of the Apostles we read that Stephen was full of grace, and that the Apostles were filled with the Holy Ghost, but their measure of grace was far other than Mary's. In her dwelt the fullness of the Godhead corporally. "Hail, full of grace, the Lord is with thee." What wonder that

---

[96] Luke 1:28

she was full of grace when the Lord was with her? Rather, is it not wonderful that He Who had sent the angel was already found by him with the Virgin? Had, then, God been swifter than the angel, and reached the earth before His messenger? Oh yes; for while the King was on His couch the spikenard of the Virgin gave forth its sweet perfume, and ascending into His glorious presence, found favour in His sight, while His ministers around exclaimed: "Who is she that goeth up by the desert, as a pillar of smoke of aromatical spices, of myrrh, and frankincense."[97] And straightway the King, going forth from His holy place, "rejoiced as a giant to run his way"[98]; and though His going out is from the height of heaven, yet through exceeding desire He hastened on His way, and anticipated His messenger with the Virgin, whom He had loved, whom He had chosen for Himself, whose beauty He had desired. Beholding Him from afar, the Church exclaims exultingly: "Behold, He cometh leaping over the mountains, skipping over the hills."[99] Rightly had the King been desirous of the Virgin's beauty, for she had long before attended to the words of her father David: "Hear, O' daughter, and see, and incline thine ear, and forget thy people and thy father's house, and the king shall desire thy beauty."[100] She heard and saw, but not as those who, hearing, hear not, and seeing, do not understand. She heard and believed, she saw and understood. She inclined her ear to obedience and her heart to discipline, and forgot her people and her father's house. She cared not

---

[97] Canticles 3:6
[98] Psalm 18:6
[99] Canticles 2:8
[100] Psalm 44:11

to multiply her people by offspring. The honour that might have been hers among her people, and the wealth that might have accrued to her from her family, she counted as dross that she might gain Christ. Not even the wish to call Christ her Son could lead her to violate her promised virginity. Truly, then, is she full of grace who clung to the grace of virginity, and also obtained the glory of fecundity.

"Hail, full of grace, the Lord is with thee." He says not *in* thee, but *with* thee. God, Who is equally present everywhere, remains whole and entire by His simple substance and essence. He is present with rational creatures in many different ways. With the good alone He is present by love as well as by knowledge, so that He is with them by agreement of wills. While their wills are subject to justice and right reason, God does not disdain to will what they will, for their wills being conformed to His, they in a manner unite God to themselves. If God is thus present with all the saints, He is especially so with Mary, with whom He was so closely united as to have not only one will, but one flesh, for from His own Divine nature and from her virginal substance one Christ was made, Who, sharing both natures, was at once the Son of God and Son of the Virgin Mary. The angel therefore says: "Hail, full of grace, the Lord is with thee." Not only is there with thee God the Son, Whom thou dost clothe with thy flesh, but also God the Holy Ghost, of Whom thou dost conceive, and God the Father, Who begot Him, Who is to be thy Son. The Father is with thee who makes His Son to be thine; the Son is with thee who institutes with thee a wondrous Sacrament, and yet preserves the seal of thy virginity. The Holy Spirit is with thee, and with the Father and the Son He sanctifies thy pure womb. "The Lord," therefore, "is with thee. Blessed art thou amongst women."

I love to add what Elizabeth soon after pronounced, and "Blessed is the fruit of thy womb." Not that, because thou art blessed, the fruit of thy womb is also blessed, but because He prevented thee with the blessings of sweetness, therefore art thou blessed. Truly blessed is the fruit of thy womb, in whom all nations are blest, of whose fullness thou hast received as others have, but in a fuller measure. For this reason, therefore, thou art blessed best "amongst women." *He* is called blessed not amongst men, nor amongst angels, but, as the Apostle says, "God blessed above all forever."[101]

"Blessed, therefore, is the fruit of thy womb"—blessed in sweet odour, blessed in sweet savour, blessed in beauty and comeliness of form.

The fragrance of this odoriferous fruit was perceived by him who said: "The smell of my son is as the smell of a plentiful field, which the Lord hath blessed"[102]; and is not he truly blessed who is blest by the Lord?

Of the sweet relish of this fruit one who had tasted of it exclaimed, "O' taste and see how sweet is the Lord"[103]; and elsewhere, "O how great is the multitude of thy sweetness, O' Lord, which thou hast hidden for them that fear thee."[104]

---

[101] Romans 9:5
[102] Genesis 27:27
[103] Psalm 33:9
[104] Psalm 30:20

And Christ says of Himself while inviting us all to Him: "He that eateth me shall yet hunger, and he that drinketh me shall yet thirst." He said this because the sweet savour of this fruit, when once tasted, excites a greater appetite. Blessed fruit! which is the food and drink of those who hunger and thirst after justice.

You have heard of its fragrance and of its savour; hear now of its beauty. For if the fruit which brought death into the world was not only sweet to the taste, but beautiful to the eye, as the Scripture testifies, much more ought we to seek for beauty in this fruit of life, "upon which," as another passage in Holy Scripture remarks, "the angels desire to look."[105] Its beauty was seen in spirit, and desired to be seen in the flesh by him who said: "Out of Zion the loveliness of his beauty."[106] And, lest you should think lightly of the beauty here commended, remember what is said in another Psalm: "Beautiful above the sons of men, grace is poured abroad on thy lips, therefore God hath blessed thee for ever." "Blessed, then, is the fruit of thy womb," whom God hath blest for ever, and by whom thou thyself, O' Mary, art blessed amongst women, because an evil tree cannot bring forth good fruit.

Blessed art thou amongst women, who didst escape that universal curse, "In sorrow thou shalt bring forth children"; and that other, "Cursed is the barren in Israel." Thou hast obtained the singular blessing of neither remaining sterile, nor bringing forth in sorrow. But who has taught thee, O' prudent

---

[105] 1 Peter 1:12
[106] Psalm 49:2

Virgin, O' devout Virgin, that virginity is pleasing to God? What page of the Old Testament exhorted thee, what ordinance counselled thee, what law commanded thee to live in the flesh, yet not according to the flesh, and lead on earth the life of the angels? Where didst thou read that the "wisdom of the flesh is death,"[107] and that we are not to "make provision for the flesh in its concupiscences"[108]? Where didst thou read of virgins that they sing a new song no other can sing, and that they follow the Lamb whithersoever He goeth? Where didst thou read that they are praised who have made themselves eunuchs for the kingdom of heaven? Where didst thou find that "though we walk in the flesh, we do not war according to the flesh"[109]; and that "he that giveth his virgin in marriage doth well; but he that giveth her not, doth better"[110]? Where didst thou hear, "I would that all men were as myself"; and "it is good for a man, if he so remain according to my counsel"? The unction of the Holy Spirit, O' Virgin, has taught thee all these things.

Before becoming thy Son God has been thy Master. Thou dost vow thyself as a chaste virgin to Christ, and thou knowest not thou shalt be His Mother. Thou wilt conceive, but without sin; thou wilt bring forth, but without sorrow; thou knowest not man, but thou wilt bear a Son. What Son? Thou wilt be Mother of Him whose Father is God. The Son of the Father's love will be the crown of thy chastity; the wisdom of

---

107 Romans 8:6
108 Romans 13:14
109 2 Corinthians 10:3
110 1 Corinthians 7:38

the Father's mind will be the fruit of thy virginal womb. Of God, therefore, thou wilt conceive, and thou wilt bring forth a God. Take courage, then, fruitful Virgin, chaste Mother, spotless Mother; thou wilt no longer be accursed in Israel, nor reckoned among the barren. Thou wilt be blessed on earth by the angel, and all generations of the earth shall call thee blessed. "Blessed art thou amongst women, and blessed is the fruit of thy womb."

"And when she had heard, she was troubled at his saying, and thought with herself what manner of salutation this might be." Virgins who deserve the name are ever timid; they never think themselves secure; and while avoiding what ought to be feared, they fear where there is no danger. They know that they bear a precious treasure in fragile vessels; that it is difficult to live among men an angelic life, to converse on earth after the manner of the celestial spirits, to lead on earth a holy life in mortal flesh. In every unforeseen occurrence they suspect some snare for their virtue, and therefore Mary was troubled at the words of the angel. She was troubled, but not disturbed. "I was troubled," says the Psalmist, "and I spoke not. I thought upon the days of old, and I had in my mind the eternal years."[111] Mary was troubled, and spoke not; she thought what manner of salutation this might be. That she was troubled proves her virginal modesty; that she was not disturbed, her fortitude; her thoughtful silence shows her prudence.

---

[111] Psalm 76:5, 6

"She thought what manner of salutation this might be." This prudent Virgin knew how often Satan transforms himself into an angel of light, and because she was singularly simple and humble, she did not expect to hear such words addressed to her by *the* angel, so she thought with herself what manner of salutation this might be. Then the angel, looking on the Virgin, and easily reading the conflicting thoughts that were passing through her mind, encouraged her in her timidity and in her doubt. Calling her by her name, he gently persuaded her not to fear.

"'Fear not, Mary, thou hast found grace with God.' There is here no deception, no falsehood. Thou needest fear no fraud, no snare, no delusion. I am not a man, but a spirit; I am an angel of God, not a minister of Satan. 'Fear not, Mary, thou hast found grace with God.' Oh, if thou didst know how pleasing thy humility is to the Most High, what a sublime exaltation awaits thee in His sight, thou wouldst not judge thyself unworthy of the conversation, nor even of the homage, of angels! Why think thyself undeserving the favour of angels when thou hast found favour with God? Thou hast found what thou hadst sought, what none before thee had been able to find—thou hast found grace before God. What grace? The grace of peace and reconciliation between God and man, the destruction of death the reparation of life. This is the grace thou hast found with God. And let this be a sign to thee. 'Thou shalt conceive and bring forth a son, and thou shalt call his name Jesus.' Understand from the name of the promised Son, O' prudent Virgin, how great and what a special grace thou hast found with God."

"And thou shalt call his name Jesus." Another Evangelist gives the reason of this name: "Because he shall save his people from their sins."[112] I have read of two men who bore the name of this our Jesus; both went before Him and prefigured Him, and both were serviceable to their people. One conducted his brethren into the Land of Promise; the other led forth his people from the captivity of Babylon. Both did, indeed, defend those they governed from their enemies, but they did not save them from their sins. But this our Jesus saves His people, and washes away their sins, and likewise introduces them into the land of the living. "For he shall save his people from their sins."

Who is this that forgiveth sins also? Would that the Lord Jesus would deign to number me, a sinner, among His people, and save me from my sins. Truly, blessed are the people that have our Lord Jesus for their God, for He will save His people from their sins. But I fear there are many who profess to be of His people, but whom He does not recognize as such. I fear that to many who are counted among the more religious-minded of His people He will say: "This people honoureth me with their lips, but their hearts are far from me."[113] For the Lord Jesus knoweth who are His, and whom He hath chosen from the beginning. "Why do you call me Lord, Lord, and do not the things I command you?"[114]

---

112 Matthew 1:21
113 Matthew 15:8; Isaiah 29:13
114 Luke 6:46

Would you know if you belong to His people, or, rather, do you wish to be one of His disciples? Do what Jesus commands, and He will number you among His followers. Fulfil what He enjoins in the Gospel, what He prescribes in the Law and the Prophets, what He ordains through His ministers in the Church. Obey His representatives; obey your superiors, not only the good and gentle, but even the froward; and learn of Jesus Himself to be meek and humble of heart. You will then belong to the blessed people whom He has chosen for His inheritance, and of whom He bears witness, saying: "A people, which I knew not, hath served me: at the hearing of the ear they have obeyed me."[115]

But let us consider what the angel thinks of Him, Whom he would willingly himself have called by the name of Jesus. He says: "He shall be great, and shall be called the Son of the Most High." Great indeed is He Who deserves to be called the Son of the Most High. Is not He great whose immensity knows no limitation? Who is great as the Lord our God? It is He Who is as great as He is high—yea, Who is Most High. As "Son of the Most High," He thought it not robbery to equal Himself to the Most High. Satan, indeed, meditated robbery. Though made out of nothing in angelic form, he compared himself with his Maker, and arrogated to himself what belonged of right to the Son of the Most High, the Son not made by God, but begotten of Him. For the Most High God the Father, though Omnipotent, could not make a creature equal to Himself, nor beget a Son who was not His equal. He

---

[115] Psalm 17:45

made the angel great, but not as Himself, therefore not Most High. In one alone did He think it no robbery that He should equal Himself with Him in all things; the only-begotten Son, Who was not made, but begotten, by the Omnipotent, Omnipotent; by the Most High, Most High; by the Eternal, Co-eternal. Rightly, then, shall He be great Who shall be called the Son of the Most High.

But why is it said "He shall be," and not, rather, "He is," great, since He is always equally great, and can have no increase? He will not be more exalted after His conception than He was before. Perhaps the angel would have us understand that He Who was great as God will be great as man. Elsewhere in the Gospel we read, "A great Prophet hath risen up amongst us."[116]

O' Virgin, thou wilt indeed give birth to a Little One, thou wilt nourish a Little One; but while thou lookest on Him as little, think upon Him as great. He will be great, because God will magnify Him in the sight of kings; wherefore let all the kings adore Him and all nations serve Him. Let thy soul magnify the Lord, for "He shall be great, and shall be called the Son of the Most High."

He shall be great; and "He that is mighty shall do great things for thee, and Holy is his name." What name holier than "Son of the Most High"? This great Lord shall be magnified also by us little ones; for He became a Little One that He might make us great. "A Child is born to us, a Son is given to

---

us."[117] "To us," not to Himself; for He Who before all ages was much more nobly born of His Father needed not in time to be born of a Mother. Nor was He born and given to the angels. They Who possessed Him in His greatness did not require Him in His lowliness. To us, then, He is born, to us He is given, because by us He is so greatly needed. And since He is born of our race and given to us, let us accomplish that for which He was born and given. Let us make use of Our Own for our profit; let us work out our salvation by means of our Saviour. Behold, "a Child is set in the midst." O' Little One, desired by little ones! O' true Child, but a guileless Child full of wisdom! Let us study to become as this Little One. Let us learn to be meek and humble of heart, lest the great God should without fruit have become Man and a Child; lest He should have died in vain and been crucified in vain. Let us learn His humility; let us imitate His meekness; let us embrace His love; let us share His sufferings; let us be washed in His blood; let us offer Him as a propitiation for our sins. To this end He was born and given to us. Let us offer Him to His Father, for the Father spared not His own Son, but delivered Him for us all; and the Son emptied Himself, taking the form of a servant, and delivered "His soul to death," and was reputed with the wicked; He bore the sins of many, and prayed for the transgressors, that they might not perish. But they cannot perish for whom the Son prays, and for whom the Father delivers His own Son to procure them life. From both, therefore, equally may we hope for pardon, because in both are equal mercy and compassion, equal power, one will, one

---

[117] Isaiah 9:6

substance in Godhead, wherein with them the Holy Ghost liveth and reigneth one God for ever and ever. Amen.

## HOMILY IV

### The Annunciation and the Blessed Virgin's Consent

**W**ho doubts that the praises we give to the Mother of God redound to the honour of the Son of God; and, in like manner, that in honouring the Son we are also honouring the Mother? For if, according to Solomon, "A wise son is the glory of the father,"[118] how much more glorious is it to become the Mother of Wisdom Himself!

But how shall I dare to commend her whose praises are announced by Prophets, spoken by an angel, recorded by the Evangelist? I will not praise, because I do not dare; I will but repeat with all devotion what the Holy Spirit Himself has spoken by the Evangelist, for the words of the text are: "And the Lord will give him the throne of David his father." These are the words of the angel to the Virgin declaring that her promised Son should possess the kingdom of David. We all know that our Lord Jesus sprang from the race of David; but how, I ask, did God give Him the throne of His father David, since He never reigned in Jerusalem? On the contrary, when the multitude desired it, He would not consent to be their King, and before Pilate He protested that His kingdom was not of this world. Besides, what great gain was it for Him

---

[118] Proverbs 10:1

Who sits upon the Cherubim, and Whom the Prophet saw "upon a throne high and elevated,"[119] to be promised the throne of His father David? But we know that another Jerusalem is signified by the Jerusalem that now is, one far nobler and richer than that in which David reigned. And I believe it to be here understood, because we often find in Scripture the figure put for that which is typified. Evidently God gave our Lord the throne of His father David when He "constituted Him King upon Zion, His holy mount."[120] And the Prophet seems to show more plainly of what kingdom he spoke when he said not *in* Zion, but *upon* Zion. David reigned *in* Zion. *Upon* Zion points out the kingdom of Him of Whom it is said to David, "Of the fruit of thy womb I will put to sit upon thy throne,"[121] and of whom another Prophet speaks, "He shall sit upon the throne of David and upon his kingdom."[122] In each text we find *upon*. "The Lord God, therefore, will give him the throne of David his father"—not a typical but a true throne, not temporal but eternal, not earthly but celestial. And what has been said above shows that David so regarded it, for the throne in which he reigned as temporal sovereign bore the image of the eternal one.

"And he shall reign over the house of Jacob for ever, and his kingdom shall have no end."[123] Here also, if we understand the temporal house of Jacob, how can we say that Christ will reign eternally, since that house is not eternal? We have

---

[119] Isaiah 6:1
[120] Psalm 2:6
[121] Psalm 131:11
[122] Isaiah 9:7
[123] Luke 1:32, 33

therefore yet to find the eternal house of Jacob in which He shall reign eternally, whose kingdom shall have no end. Question the Apostle, and he will point out to you the difference between him who is a Jew inwardly and him who is only outwardly a Jew; between the circumcision of the spirit and the circumcision which is only of the flesh[124]—that is, between the spiritual and the carnal Jew, the children of the faith of Abraham and the children according to the flesh. "For all are not Israelites that are of Israel. Neither are all they that are of the seed of Abraham, children."[125] In like manner we may look upon those alone who are found perfect in the faith of Jacob, or Israel, as constituting the spiritual and eternal house of Jacob in which the Lord Jesus shall reign eternally.

Who is there amongst us who, according to the interpretation of the name Jacob, makes Jesus Christ supplant the devil in his heart? Who is there that struggles with his vices and concupiscences that sin may not reign in his mortal body, but that in him Jesus may reign, now, indeed, by grace, afterwards eternally by glory? Blessed are they in whom Jesus shall reign eternally, for they also shall reign with Him, and of His kingdom there shall be no end. Oh, how glorious is that kingdom in which Kings have assembled, and have agreed together to praise and glorify Him Who is King of Kings and Lord of Lords; in the glorious contemplation of Whom the just shall shine as the sun in the kingdom of their Father! Oh, may our Lord Jesus deign to be mindful of me, a sinner, when

---

[124] Colossians 2:11
[125] Romans 9:6, 7

He cometh in His kingdom. In that day when He shall give up His kingdom into the hands of God and the Father, may He graciously visit me in His saving mercy, may He look on me in goodness as one of His elect, may He rejoice me with the joy of His chosen people, and be praised even by me with all His inheritance! Come, Lord Jesus, take away scandals from Thy kingdom, which is my soul, and reign therein, Thou Who alone hast the right. For avarice comes to claim a throne within me; haughtiness and self-assertion would rule over me; pride would be my king; luxury says, "I will reign"; ambition, detraction, envy, and anger struggle within me for the mastery. I resist as far as I am able; I struggle according as help is given me; I call on my Lord Jesus; for His sake I defend myself, since I acknowledge myself as wholly His possession. He is my God; Him alone I cling to, Him I proclaim my Lord; I have no other King than my Lord Jesus Christ. Come, then, O' Lord, and disperse these enemies in Thy power, and Thou shalt reign in me, for Thou Thyself art my King and my God, Who gives salvation to Thy chosen ones.

"But Mary said to the angel: How shall this be done, because I know not man?" At first she kept a prudent silence, for she was in doubt what this salutation might be, and she preferred in humility to give no answer rather than risk speaking of what she did not understand. Now, however, she was strengthened and prepared, for while the angel spoke externally God disposed her heart, for the Lord was present with her when the angel said, "The Lord is with thee."

Thus animated to cast out fear by a spirit of faith, she said to the angel: "How shall this be done, for I know not man?" She doubts not the fact, but only inquires about the manner of its accomplishment. She says not "*Will* it be done?" but "*How* will this be done?" As if she would say: "Since my Lord knows, and my conscience bears me witness, that His handmaid has made a vow to know no man, by what law shall it please Him to work this wonder? If I must break my vow that I may bring forth such a Son, I rejoice on account of the Son, but I grieve because of my vow. Nevertheless, His will be done. If, however, as a Virgin I may bring forth this Son— and it is not impossible if He so will it—then I shall know that He hath had regard to the humility of His handmaid. How, then, shall this be done, for I know not man?"

"And the angel, answering, said to her: The Holy Ghost shall come upon thee, and the power of the Most High shall overshadow thee." It had been said before that she was full of grace; how is it now said: "The Holy Ghost shall come upon thee, and the power of the Most High shall overshadow thee"? Could she be filled with grace and not possess the Holy Spirit, the giver of all grace? And if He is already in her, how is it promised that He shall come upon her in some new way? Was it not to explain this to us that the angel said not merely "*in* thee," but also "*upon* thee"? For the Holy Spirit was in her before His coming by an abundant grace; now it is declared that He will *come upon* her by the fullness of the more abundant grace which He will pour out upon her.

But how will she be able to receive a fresh infusion of Divine grace when she is already full of grace? And if she can receive more, how are we to understand that she is already full of grace? Was it that hitherto grace had only filled her mind and soul, and that the new infusion of it was to penetrate her body, so that the plenitude of the Divinity which had hitherto dwelt in her spiritually—as He dwells in many of the saints—might begin to abide in her corporeally as He has never dwelt in any other saint? Yes, this is what the angel reveals to us. "The Holy Ghost shall come upon thee, and the power of the Most High shall overshadow thee."

"And therefore also the Holy One which shall be born of thee shall be called the Son of God." That is to say, "Since it is not of man, but of the Holy Ghost, that you conceive, and since you conceive by the Power of the Most High, therefore what is born of thee is holy, and shall be called the Son of God." In like manner, "He Who was born of the Father before all ages will also be called your Son. What was born of the Father shall be thine; what shall be born of thee shall be His; yet there will not be two Sons, but one Son," and "therefore the Holy One that shall be born of thee shall be called the Son of God."

"And behold thy cousin Elizabeth, she also hath conceived a son in her old age." Why was it necessary to make known this event to the Blessed Virgin? Had she been doubtful or incredulous of the angel's words? Far from it. We read that the hesitation of Zachary was punished by this same angel, but we do not read that Mary received the least blame; on the contrary, we know that her faith was praised by Elizabeth: "Blessed art thou that hast believed, because those things shall be accomplished that were spoken to thee by the Lord." Her cousin's happiness was announced to Mary that, miracle being added to miracle, joy might be heaped upon joy. For it was needful that no ordinary prevenient joy and burning love should take possession of her who, with the joy of the Holy Ghost, was soon to conceive the Son of the Father's love. A most glad and most generous heart was alone capable of containing so exuberant an influx of sweetness and delight.

Again, the announcement may have been made to Mary, in order that she might be cognizant, not only of the Saviour's coming, but also of His precursors, and that, by preserving a faithful remembrance of the order and circumstances of the events, she might later be better able to unfold the truth of the Gospel to those who were to write and preach it. This was the rightful office of her who from the first had been fully instructed by Heaven in all its secret mysteries. Or we may believe that Mary was told of Elizabeth's happiness to give her, the younger of the two, the opportunity of tendering her loving service to her cousin, and that the little unborn Prophet might offer to his younger Lord the first-fruits of his ministry, while the joy and devotion of both infants being excited by the meeting and mutual joy of the mothers, wonder might be added to wonder, miracle to miracle.

Lest, however, it should be supposed that the accomplishment of these magnificent promises was brought about by the angel who declares them, he adds: "For no word shall be impossible to God." As if he would say: "In all that I faithfully promise I rest not on my own power, but on the power of Him Who sent me, for no word shall be impossible with Him." How could any word be impossible to Him Who made all things by the Word? And this is striking—that the angel expressly says no *word* shall be impossible, not no *act*. He says *word* because, as men can easily speak what they wish, even though they cannot afterwards carry it into effect, with the same or, rather, with incomparably greater facility can God accomplish in act what they are able to express in words; therefore with good reason "no word is impossible with God." For instance, the Prophets by God's power could foresee and predict that a virgin and a barren woman would have sons; but God alone, Who enabled the Prophets to foresee these events, could by His own power fulfil what He had promised. Because, too, He is Infinite Power and Infinite Wisdom, "no word shall be impossible with" Him.

You have heard, O' Virgin, the announcement of the great mystery; the means designed for its fulfilment have been unfolded to you, each wondrous, each replete with joy. "Rejoice, O' daughter of Zion, and exult exceedingly, O' virgin daughter of Jerusalem." And because to you has been given joy and gladness, allow us to hear from your lips the answer and the good tidings which we desire, that the bones that have been humbled may rejoice. You have heard the fact, and have believed; believe also in the means which have been explained to you. You have heard that you are to conceive and bring forth a Son, and that it will not be through the power of man, but by the virtue of the Holy Ghost.

The angel awaits your reply, for it is time that he should return to God, Who sent him. We, too, are waiting, O' Lady, for a word of mercy—we, who are groaning under the sentence of condemnation. See, the price of our salvation is offered to you; if you consent, we shall at once be delivered. By the Eternal Word of God we were all created, and behold we die. By your short answer we shall be refreshed and recalled to life. Adam, with all his race—Adam, a weeping exile from Paradise, implores it of you. Abraham entreats you, David beseeches you. This is the object of the burning desires of the holy fathers, of *your* fathers, who are still dwelling in the region of the shades of death. Behold the entire human race prostrate at your feet in expectation.

And rightly, for on your word depend the consolation of the wretched, the redemption of the captive, the freedom of the condemned, the salvation of your entire race, of all the children of Adam. Hasten, then, O' Lady, to give your answer; hasten to speak the word so longed for by all on earth, in limbo, and in heaven. Yea, the King and Lord of all things, Who has greatly desired your beauty, desires as eagerly your word of consent, by which He has purposed to save the world. He whom you have pleased by your silence will now be more gratified by your reply.

Hark! He calls to you from heaven: "O' most beautiful among women, give me to hear your voice." If you let Him hear your voice, He will enable you to see our salvation. And is not this what you have sought for, what you have prayed for night and day with sighs and tears? Why, then, delay? Are you the happy one to whom it has been promised, or "look we for another"? Yes, you indeed are that most fortunate one. You are the promised virgin, the expected virgin, the much-longed-for virgin, through whom your holy father Jacob, when about to die, rested his hope of eternal life, saying: "I will look for thy salvation, O' Lord."[126]

You, O' Mary, are that virgin in whom and by whom God Himself, our King before all ages, determined to operate our salvation in the midst of the earth. Why do you humbly expect from another what is offered to you, and will soon be manifested through yourself if you will but yield your consent and speak the word? Answer, then, quickly to the angel—yes, through the angel give your consent to your God. Answer the word, receive the Word. Utter yours, conceive the Divine. Speak the word that is transitory, and embrace the Word that is everlasting.

Why do you delay? Why are you fearful? Believe—confess—receive. Let humility put on courage, and timidity confidence. It is certainly by no means fitting that virginal simplicity should forget prudence. Yet in this one case only the prudent virgin need not fear presumption, because, though modesty shone forth in her silence, it is now more necessary that her devotion and obedience should be revealed by her speech.

Open, O' Blessed Virgin, your heart to faith, your lips to compliance, your bosom to your Creator. Behold, the desired

---

of all nations stands at the gate and knocks. Oh, suppose He were to pass by while you delay! How would you begin again with sorrow to seek Him whom your soul loveth! Arise— run—open! Arise by faith, run by devotion, open by acceptance. *Mary speaks*. "Behold the handmaid of the Lord, may it be done unto me according to thy word."

Humility is ever the close companion of Divine grace, for "God resisteth the proud, and giveth grace to the humble." She answers humbly, therefore, that the throne of grace may be prepared. "Behold the handmaid of the Lord." She is the chosen Mother of God, and she calls herself His handmaid. Truly, it is no small sign of humility to preserve even the remembrance of the virtue in presence of so great glory. It is no great perfection to be humble when we are despised; but it is a great and rare virtue to preserve humility in the midst of honours. If, deceived by my apparent virtue, the Church has raised me, an insignificant man, to some small dignity, God permitting it, either because of my own sins, or those of my subjects, do I not immediately, forgetting my past deficiencies, imagine myself to be that which men, who see not the heart, have reputed me to be? I hearken to fame, and attend not to conscience. I forget that honour is rendered to virtue, and take the virtue for granted because of the honour, and so esteem myself the more holy when I find myself in an exalted position. Let us listen to the words of her who, though chosen to be the Mother of God, yet laid not aside her humility. "Behold," she says, "the handmaid of the Lord, may it be done unto me according to thy word."

*Fiat mihi* (Be it done to me). *Fiat* is a mark of desire, not of doubt. In saying, "Be it done unto me according to thy word," she expresses the disposition of one who longs to see the effect, not of one who doubts its possibility. *Fiat* may also be understood as a word of petition, for no one prays unless he believes, and hopes to obtain. God wishes to be asked for what He has promised, and perhaps promises many things which He had predetermined to bestow, in order that the promise may arouse our devotion, and that what He intends to give gratis we may merit by devout prayer. Thus, our gracious God, Who desires the salvation of all, as it were, extorts meritorious works from us, and while He strengthens our will by His grace, He wishes that what He gives freely we shall labour to obtain.

This the prudent Virgin understood when to the prevenient grace of a gratuitous promise she joined the merit of her own prayer, saying: "Be it done unto me according to thy word."

Be it done unto me concerning the Divine Word according to Thy word. May the Word which was in the beginning with God be made flesh of my flesh according to Thy word. May He, I entreat, be made to me, not a spoken word, to pass unheeded, but a word conceived—that is, clothed in flesh— which may remain. May He be to me not only audible to my ears, but visible to my eyes, felt by my hands, borne in my arms. Let Him be to me not a mute and written word traced with dumb signs on lifeless parchments, but an Incarnate, living Word vividly impressed in human form in my chaste womb by the operation of the Holy Ghost.

Be it done unto me as it has never hitherto been done to mortal, and never shall be done to any after my time. "God diversely and in many ways spoke in times past to the fathers by the prophets"[127]—to some in the hearing of the ears, while to others the word of the Lord was made known in signs and figures. Now in this solemn hour I pray that in my own being it may be done unto me according to Thy word.

Be it done unto me—not preached to me in the feeble strains of human eloquence, not shown forth to me in the figures of earthly rhetoric, not painted in the poetic dreams of a fervid imagination, but breathed upon me in silence, in person Incarnate, in a human form veritably reposing within me. In His own nature the Word needed not change, was incapable of change. Yet now graciously in me "may it be done according to thy word." Be it done universally for all mankind, but most especially for me—"Be it done unto me according to thy word."

---

[127] Hebrews 1:1

# III

# ON THE VIGIL OF OUR LORD'S NATIVITY

I

## On the Joy His Birth Should Inspire

"The voice of gladness hath resounded in our land, the voice of exultation and salvation in the tents of sinners. A good word has been heard, a consoling word, a speech full of joyfulness, a rumour worthy of all acceptance. Sing praise, O' ye mountains, and all ye trees of the woods. Clap your hands before the face of the Lord, because He cometh. Hear, O' ye heavens, and give ear, O' earth! Be amazed, and let every creature give praise; but thou beyond others, O' man!"[128]

## Jesus Christ, the Son of God, is born in Bethlehem of Judah.

What heart so stony as not to be softened at these words? What soul is not melted at this voice of her Beloved? What announcement could be sweeter? what intelligence more enrapturing? Was its like ever heard before? or when did the world ever receive such tidings?

## Jesus Christ, the Son of God, is born in Bethlehem of Judah.

O' short word, telling of the Eternal Word abbreviated for us! O' word full of heavenly delights! The heart is oppressed by its mellifluous sweetness, and longs to pour forth its

---

[128] Jeremiah 33:11

redundant riches, but words refuse their service. So overpowering is the music of this short speech that it loses melody if one iota is changed.

## Jesus Christ, the Son of God, is born in Bethlehem of Judah.

O' Nativity of spotless sanctity! O' birth honourable for the world, birth pleasing and welcome to men, because of the magnificence of the benefit it bestows; birth incomprehensible to the angels, by reason of the depth and sacredness of the mystery! In all its circumstances it is wonderful because of its singular excellence and novelty. Its precedent has not been known, nor has its like ever followed. O' birth alone without sorrow, alone without shame, free from corruption, not unlocking, but consecrating the temple of the Virgin's womb! O' Nativity above nature, yet for the sake of nature! Surpassing it by the excellence of the miracle, repairing it by the virtue of the mystery! Who shall declare this generation? The angel announces it. Almighty Power overshadows it. The Spirit of the Most High comes upon it. The Virgin believes. By faith she conceives. The Virgin brings forth. The Virgin remains a virgin. Who is not filled with astonishment? The Son of the Most High is born. The Son, begotten of God before all ages, is Incarnate! The Word is become an Infant! Who can sufficiently admire?

And it is not a needless Nativity, a superfluous condescension of Infinite Majesty.

## Jesus Christ, the Son of God, is born in Bethlehem of Judah.

Awake, you who lie in the dust—awake and give praise. Behold, the Lord cometh with salvation. He comes with salvation, He comes with unction, He comes with glory. Jesus cannot come without salvation, Christ cannot come without unction, nor the Son of God without glory. For He Himself is salvation, He is unction, He is glory, as it is written, "A wise son is the glory of his father."[129]

Happy the soul who has tasted this fruit of salvation, and is drawn to "run in the odour of his ointments,"[130] that she may "see his glory, the glory as of the only-begotten of the Father." Take courage, you who were lost: Jesus comes to seek and save that which was lost. Ye sick, return to health: Christ comes to heal the contrite of heart with the unction of His mercy. Rejoice, all you who desire great things: the Son of God comes down to you that He may make you the co-heirs of His kingdom. I beseech you, then, O' Lord, heal me, and I shall be healed; save me, and I shall be saved; glorify me, and I shall be glorious. Then indeed shall my soul bless the Lord, and all that is within me praise His Holy Name, when He shall have been merciful to my iniquities, have healed my infirmities, and have filled my desire with good things.

On account of these three precious gifts of salvation, unction, and glory, it is consoling to hear that Jesus Christ, the Son of God, is born. For why is He called Jesus, but

---

[129] Proverbs 10:1
[130] Canticles 1:3

because He shall save His people from their sins? Why has He willed to be named Christ, but because He will soften the yoke of His law by the unction of His grace? Why was the Son of God made man, but to make men the sons of God? Who shall resist His will? If Jesus justifies, who can condemn? If Christ heals, who can wound? If the Son of God exalts, who shall cast us down?

Since *Jesus* is born, let everyone rejoice whom the consciousness of sin has condemned as deserving of eternal punishment. For the compassion of Jesus exceeds all crimes, however great their number and enormity. Since *Christ* is born, let him rejoice who wages war with the vices inherent in our nature. No disorder of the soul, how inveterate soever, can withstand the unction which Christ brings. Since the *Son of God* is born, let him rejoice who desires great things, for a great rewarder comes. "This is the heir"; let us receive Him devoutly, "and the inheritance shall be ours." For He Who has given us His own Son, how has He not with Him given us all things? Let no one disbelieve, let no one doubt; we have a most trustworthy testimony. "The Word was made flesh and dwelt amongst us."

The only-begotten Son of God desired to have brethren, that He might be the first among many brethren. Even human frailty has no cause to hesitate. He has become the brother of men; He has become the Son of man; He has become man. "Et Homo factus est." And, if man thinks this incredible, sense enforces belief.

## Jesus Christ, the Son of God, is born in Bethlehem of Judah.

Behold what condescension! It is not in the royal city of Jerusalem, but in Bethlehem, which is the least of the thousands of Judah. O' Bethlehem! O' little Bethlehem! once little, now magnified by the Lord! He has magnified thee Who, though great, became little in thee.

Rejoice, O' Bethlehem, and make holiday in thy streets with songs of Alleluia! What city on hearing of thy good fortune will not envy thee that most precious stable and the glory of its manger? In all the wide world thy name is now celebrated, and all generations call thee blessed. Everywhere glorious things are said of thee, O' little city of God. Everywhere is sung, "A man is born in her, and the Most High himself hath founded her."[131] Everywhere it is proclaimed, everywhere it is made known that

## Jesus Christ, the Son of God, is born in Bethlehem of Judah.

Nor is it idly added "of Judah." This word reminds us of God's promise to our fathers. "The sceptre shall not be taken from Judah, nor the leader from his thigh, until he come who is to be sent, and he shall be the expectation of nations." "For salvation is of the Jews;"[132]"salvation to the ends of the earth."[133] To Judah Jacob says: "Thee shall thy brethren praise:

---

[131] Psalm 86:3, 5
[132] John 4:22
[133] Acts 13:47; Isaiah 49:6

thy hands shall be on the necks of thy enemies."[134] All these words we see fulfilled in Christ, Who, ascending on high, led captivity captive, yet derived no earthly advantage therefrom, but rather gave gifts to men. These and similar prophecies are recalled to the mind by the words "Bethlehem of Judah."

And we have no need to inquire whether anything good can come from Bethlehem; it is sufficient for us to know that our Lord willed to be born there. For doubtless there were in the world noble palaces which He might have judged worthy of His choice—palaces where the King of Glory might have been received more honourably; but it was not to purchase them that He came from His royal throne. In his left hand were riches and glory; in His right hand length of days.[135] There was an endless supply of these treasures in heaven, but poverty could not be found there. Earth abounded and superabounded in this kind of merchandise, and men knew not its value. The Son of God was desirous of it. He came down from heaven to make it His own, and so render it precious to us by His choice. Adorn thy bridal-chamber, O' Zion, O' devout soul, but with humility, but with poverty. These are the swathing-bands that please our Infant Jesus; these are the rich robes in which Mary tells us He loves to be clothed. Sacrifice to thy God the abominations of the Egyptians.

Remember, too, that it is in Bethlehem of Judah that Jesus is born; and be very careful lest you fail to be found there, lest

---

[134] Genesis 49:8
[135] Proverbs 3:16

He fail to be received by you. Bethlehem is the house of bread; Judah signifies confession or praise. If, then, you replenish your soul with the food of the Divine Word, the Body of our Lord Jesus Christ, and devoutly receive the Bread which came down from heaven, and which giveth life to the world; if the vessel of your body is made strong and able to hold the new wine by being refreshed and strengthened with His new and glorified flesh; if, moreover, you live by faith, and have no need to weep because you have forgotten to eat your bread, then, indeed, you are become a Bethlehem fitted to receive our Lord.

But see that praise be not wanting. Put on praise and beauty; these are the garments Christ approves of in those who serve Him. The Apostle commends them to you in a few words: "In the heart we believe unto justice; by the mouth is made confession unto salvation."[136] Let, then, justice be in the heart, the justice which is of faith. This alone has glory before God. Let confession also be in the mouth unto salvation, and you are sure to receive Him Who was born in Bethlehem of Judah, Jesus Christ the Son of God.


## II

### On the Miraculous Nature of the Nativity

The custom of our Order does not demand a sermon to-day; but as to-morrow we shall be engaged longer than usual in the

---

[136] Romans 10:10

celebration of the Masses, and the short remaining time will not allow of a long sermon, I thought it would not be out of place to prepare your hearts to-day for so great a festival. It is the more permissible as the mystery of this day is so profound and so incomprehensible. It is a fountain of life whose waters can never be exhausted—waters that flow the more plentifully the more freely they are drawn. I know, too, how great are your sufferings and tribulations for Christ's sake, and glad should I be that your comfort might also abound through Him. Worldly consolation is what I am neither willing nor permitted to offer. Such a consolation is both useless and valueless—yea, it is a thing to be dreaded, for it is a true hindrance to the consolation which is from heaven. For this reason He Who is the delight and glory of the angels is become the salvation and the consolation of all who suffer. He Who is glorious and transcendent in His own city, and beatifies its citizens by His presence, became little and humble, when in exile, that He might rejoice the exiles. He Who in the highest heavens is the glory of the Father became, as a Child on earth, "peace to men of good will."

A Little One is given to little ones, that the Great One may be given to the great, and that those whom the Little One justifies, the Great and Mighty One may afterwards magnify and render glorious. Hence, without doubt, St. Paul, the vessel of election, pours out to us the treasures which he had received from the fullness of this Child. For Christ, though a Child, is full of grace and truth. "In Him dwelleth all the fullness of the Godhead corporally." Hence, I repeat, St. Paul utters that good word which you have heard so often during these past days: "Rejoice in the Lord always: again I say, Rejoice." Of the showing forth of the mystery, he says "Rejoice"[137]; of the promise of it he adds: "Again I say, Rejoice." For both the mystery and its promise are causes of great joy. Rejoice that you have received the gifts of the left hand; rejoice in the expectation of the rewards of the right. "His left hand is under my head, and his right hand shall embrace me."[138] For the left hand raises, the right receives. The left hand heals and justifies; the right embraces and blesses. In the left hand are contained His merits, in the right His rewards. In the right are delights, in the left are remedies.

But see how gentle the Physician is! behold how wise! Consider diligently the novelty of these remedies that He brings. See how they are not merely precious, but beautiful as well. They are fruits beneficial for our healing, and at the same time they are charming to the spiritual eye, sweet to the spiritual taste.

Notice, I beg of you, that His first remedy is in His left hand; this is His conception without human co-operation. How new, how wonderful, how attractive is this gift! For what is fairer than the chaste generation; what more glorious than a holy and pure conception in which there is no shame, no stain, no corruption?

"Behold," He says, "I make all things new." Who is it that so speaks? It is no other than the Lamb Who sitteth upon the throne—the Lamb all sweetness, the Lamb all happiness, the

---

<sup>137</sup> Philippians 4:4
<sup>138</sup> Canticles 2:6

Lamb all unction; for His name is Christ. O' miraculous novelty! The curse of Eve is reversed in our Virgin, for she brought forth her Son without pain or sorrow. The curse has been changed into a blessing, as the Angel Gabriel foretold: "Blessed art thou amongst women." O' only blessed one amongst women! Blest, not cursed! Alone free from the universal malediction! And no wonder that Jesus gave no sorrow to His Mother, since He Himself bore all the sorrows of the world, as Isaiah says: "Truly he hath carried our sorrows."[139]

There are two things from which our weak human nature shrinks—pain and shame. Christ came to take both from us, and this He did by accepting both in His own person—when, for instance, not to mention other occasions, He was condemned to death, and to a most shameful death, by wicked men. And, to give us fullest confidence of this deliverance, He first freed His Mother from both. This is an unheard-of wonder, yet we see here still greater miracles and still fuller glory. The Mother loses not her virginity, the Son is without stain of sin. The curse of Eve falls not on the Mother, nor is the Son subject to the universal calamity of which the Prophet speaks: "No one is clean, not even the babe whose life upon earth is but one day." Behold here an Infant without stain! Behold the Lamb without spot, the Lamb of God, Who taketh away the sins of the world! Who could better take them away than He Who knew no sin? He, indeed, can cleanse me, who has never Himself been defiled. His

---

<sup>139</sup> Isaiah 53:4

touch can remove the clay from my eyes, for His hand is free from the lightest dust. He can take the mote from out my eye Who has no beam in His own; or, rather, He Who has no smallest grain of dust in His own eye can take the beam from mine.

We have now certainly seen the riches of salvation and of life. We have seen His glory, the glory as of the Only-begotten of the Father. What Father? "And he shall be called the Son of the Most High."[140] "That which shall be born of thee shall be holy, and shall be called the Son of God."

Oh, truly the Holy One! Here miracles increase in number, riches are multiplied, a treasure is opened out. Our treasure was hidden. The incorruption of the Mother was hidden in the legal purification, and the innocence of the Child in the customary circumcision. Hide, O' Mary, hide the brightness of the new Sun; place Him in the manger, wrap your Infant in swaddling-clothes, for His swathing-bands are our riches. The rags of our Saviour are more precious than purple, and His poor manger is more glorious than the gilded thrones of kings. The poverty of Christ is greater riches than all this world's wealth, for what is richer or more precious than the humility by which heaven is bought and Divine grace is obtained? "Blessed are the poor in spirit, for theirs is the kingdom of heaven." And St. James says: "God resists the proud, and gives his grace to the humble."[141]

---

[140] Luke 1:32
[141] James 4:6

We see humility commended in our Lord's Nativity, for in it "he emptied himself, taking the form of a servant, and in habit was found as man." If you desire to find yet greater riches, yet higher glory, behold His charity in His passion; for "greater love than this no man hath, that he lay down his life for his friends." These riches of salvation are the precious blood in which we were redeemed. This glory is the cross of our Lord, so that with the Apostle we exclaim, "God forbid that I should glory, save in the cross of my Lord Jesus Christ"[142]; and elsewhere: "I have not judged myself to know anything among you, but Jesus Christ and him crucified."[143] This is the "left hand," Jesus Christ and Him crucified; the "right hand" is Jesus Christ and Him glorified. Show us, O' Lord, Thy right hand, and it is sufficient for us, for "at thy right hand are delights even to the end."[144] "Glory and wealth shall be in the house of him that feareth the Lord."[145]

What, then, shall be found in *Thy* house? Oh, it will be thanksgiving and the voice of praise. "Blessed are they that dwell in thy house, O' Lord: they shall praise thee for ever and ever."[146] "Eye hath not seen, nor ear heard, neither hath it entered into the heart of man, what things God hath prepared for them that love him." They are light inaccessible, peace which surpasseth all understanding, a stream of delights ceaselessly flowing. Eye hath not seen light inaccessible, ear hath not heard what is peace incomprehensible. "How

---

[142] Galatians 6:14
[143] 1 Corinthians 2:2
[144] Psalms 15:2
[145] Psalms 113:2
[146] Psalms 84:4

beautiful are the feet of them that preach the gospel of peace."[147] But though their sound "hath gone forth into all the earth," it hath surpassed all their understanding to comprehend how deep is this peace; they could not, therefore, transmit it to other ears. "Ear hath not heard it." St. Paul himself says: "Brethren, I count not myself to have apprehended."[148] But faith cometh by hearing, and hearing by the Word of God—yes, faith, not vision; the promise of peace, not its manifestation. It is true even now there is peace upon earth to men of good-will. But what is this peace compared to that plenitude and abundance of peace to be enjoyed in God's house? Whence our Lord says, "Peace I leave with you, my peace I give you."[149] *My* peace—that is, the peace which surpasseth all understanding, and is peace upon peace. You are not able to receive it yet, therefore I promise you the country of peace, and "leave" you in the meantime the way of peace.

"Neither hath it entered into the heart of man what things God hath prepared for them that love him."[150] Why cannot the thought of the good things God has prepared for us enter into our hearts? Is it that pride lifts up the heart and grace cannot flow in? It would seem so, for every proud spirit, like Satan, exalts itself above God. God wishes His will to be done; the proud man prefers to do his own. What folly! God desires His will to be carried out only in those things which

---

[147] Isaiah 52:7; Romans 10:15
[148] Philippians 3:13
[149] John 14:27
[150] 1 Corinthians 2:9

reason approves; the proud man will have his will accomplished without reason, and even contrary to reason. This is a height to which the streams of grace cannot rise. "Unless you be converted, and become as this little child," says our Lord, "you shall not enter into the kingdom of heaven." He is Himself the little and humble Child whom He sets for our Model. He is the Fountain of life, in whom dwelleth and from whom floweth the fullness of all grace. Prepare, then, the way for the waters of grace. Cast down the heights of earthly and proud thoughts. Be conformed to the Son of man, not to the first and fallen man, for the streams of grace cannot "enter into" the heart of the proud and carnal— that is, of the earthly-minded man. Cleanse your "eye," that you may be capable of beholding the most pure light of faith. Incline your "ear" to the call of obedience, that you may one day attain to perpetual rest and peace upon peace. That future life is called "light" because of its serenity, peace because of its tranquillity, a fountain because of its abundance and its eternity.

We may attribute the "fountain "to the Father, of Whom the Son is born, and from Whom the Holy Ghost proceeds; "light" to the Son, Who is the brightness of eternal life, and the true light enlightening every man who cometh into this world; "peace," to the Holy Ghost, Who rests upon the humble and peaceable. I do not mean to say that these names are proper to any of the three Divine Persons, for the Father is Light, since the Son is Light of Light; and the Son is Peace, as the Apostle says, "he is our peace who hath made both one"[151]; and the Holy Ghost is the "Fountain of Water springing up into life everlasting."[152]

But when shall we attain to these wonderful truths? When, O' Lord, wilt Thou fill us with joy by the sight of Thy countenance? We rejoice in Thee that Thou, the Orient from on high, hast visited us. We rejoice, too, "in the blessed hope" of Thy second coming.

But when shall come that fullness of joy not in the memory of past blessings, but in actual possession of the eternal—joy, not in the expectation of good things, but in their present manifestation? "Behold," He says, "I am with you all days, even to the end of the world."[153] "The Lord is nigh, be nothing solicitous."[154] He is at hand, and will soon appear. Faint not; be not weary. "Seek him while he may be found, call upon him while he is near." He is near to them who are of a contrite heart; He is near to those who wait for Him, who expect Him in truth.

Would you likewise know how near He is? Listen to the song of the Spouse to her Divine Bridegroom: "Behold, he standeth behind our wall."[155] This wall is our mortal body, which hinders our seeing Him Who is so near, and it is the reason why St. Paul himself desires "to be dissolved and to be with Christ"; and, crying out yet more piteously, he says: "Unhappy man that I am, who will deliver me from the body

---

[151] Ephesians 2:14
[152] John 4:14
[153] Matthew 28:20
[154] Philippians 4:5
[155] Song of Solomon 2:9

of this death?"[156] The Prophet also speaks in the Psalm: "Lead my soul out of prison, that I may praise thy name."[157]

# III

## On the Dispositions Required in Those Who Celebrate the Feast

"We have heard a rumour from the Lord, and he hath sent an ambassador to the nations."[158]

**W**e have heard a rumour full of grace, worthy of all acceptance. "Jesus Christ, the Son of God, is born in Bethlehem of Judah." My soul is melted at this word, and my spirit burns within me through eager desire to proclaim it to you. *Jesus* is, interpreted, Saviour. What so necessary to the lost? What so desirable to the wretched? What so welcome to the hopeless? Without this gracious promise, whence should we have obtained redemption? Unless some new and unexpected help had arisen for us, how could we have had the faintest hope of salvation, subject as we were and are to a law of sin, living in a body of death, surrounded by the wickedness of this present life, which is only a place of affliction? Perhaps you will tell me that you do desire salvation, you do desire a cure, but that, knowing your own weakness, you shrink from the sharpness of the remedy. Fear not. Christ is all sweetness

---

[156] Romans 7:24
[157] Psalms 141:8
[158] Abdias 1:1

and gentleness. He is full of mercy, for He is "anointed with the oil of gladness beyond his fellows"—that is, beyond those who enjoy at least a share of that unction, though they do not receive it in its plenitude.

When, however, you hear that Jesus is sweet and gentle, do not suppose Him a weak and inefficient Saviour, for He is the "Son of God." Such as the Father is, such is the Son. He has the power to do whatever He wills. Had your Saviour been an angel, or an archangel, or anyone from the higher orders of blessed spirits, you would have had no cause for discontent. Since, however, He is one Who has inherited a much more excellent name than they—Jesus Christ, the Son of God—He ought to be received with all devotion.

And notice that Gabriel commended these His titles clearly when he announced "a great joy" to the shepherds, for he said: "This day is born to you a Saviour, Who is Christ the Lord." Let us, then, exult and repeatedly rejoice in this birth, because it so convincingly persuades us of the usefulness of salvation, of the sweetness of the anointing, and of the majesty of the Son of God that nothing is wanted to its glory.

Let us rejoice as we ponder upon this sweet message. Let us repeat to one another this delightful speech: "Jesus Christ, the Son of God, is born in Bethlehem of Judah." Let no one be so indevout, so ungrateful, so irreligious, as to say: This is nothing new; it was heard long ago; Christ was born long ago. I answer: Yes, long ago and before long ago. No one will be surprised at my words if he remembers that expression of the Prophet, *In æternum et ultra*, "for ever and ever," or, "for ever and beyond it." Christ, then, is born not only before our times, but before all time. That Nativity made "darkness its hiding-place," or, more truly, "it abides in light inaccessible"; it hides in the bosom of the Father as in the "thick and shady mountain." Therefore, that this mysterious Nativity might to some extent be made known, Jesus Christ was born in time, born of flesh, born in flesh, "the Word was made flesh."

What wonder, then, if to-day the Church says, "Christ, the Son of God, is born," when so long before it had been said of Him, "A Child is born to us"! This word began to be heard in the ancient days, and none of the saints of the old law ever grew weary of its repetition. So that we may say, "Jesus Christ yesterday, to-day, and the same for ever."

God revealed this His secret counsel to the man "according to his own heart"—the man to whom "he swore truth, and he will not make it void: Of the fruit of thy womb I will set upon thy throne."[159] For this reason it is that He is born in Bethlehem of Judah, in the city of David—that is, for the sake of God's truth and to confirm the promises made to the Fathers. This birth was "at sundry times and in divers manners spoken of in times past to the fathers by the prophets."[160]

Hearing of this birth of our Saviour, is there one amongst us who does not say in his heart, "It is good for me to adhere to my God,"[161] or those other words of the same Prophet,

---

159 Psalm 131:11
160 Hebrews 1:1
161 Psalm 72:28

"Shall not my soul be subject to God?"[162] In this day's most joyful announcement it is not said "*has been* born," but "*is* born"; it is not treated as a past event, but as one actually taking place. "Jesus Christ, the Son of God, is born in Bethlehem of Judah." For, as He continues still to be in a manner immolated daily whilst we announce His death, so He seems to be born again while we devoutly commemorate His Nativity.

To-morrow, therefore, we shall see the majesty of God, but with us, amongst us, not in Himself. We shall see Majesty in humility, Power in weakness, the God-man. For He is Emmanuel—"God with us"—and "the Word was made flesh, and dwelt amongst us." Finally, from that time and ever since "we have seen his glory, the glory as of the only-begotten of the Father"—a glory, therefore, "full of grace and truth."[163]

He is born, then—but where? In Bethlehem of Judah. It would ill become us to leave Bethlehem unnoticed. "Let us go over to Bethlehem," say the shepherds. They do not say, "Let us pass by Bethlehem." What though it be a little town? What if it does seem to be the least in Judea? Is not such a town becoming for Him Who, "being rich, became poor for our sake," and Who, though He was the "Lord great and exceedingly to be praised," was born for us a Little One, and said, "Blessed are the poor in spirit, for theirs is the kingdom of heaven"? Therefore He chose a stable and a manger—yea, a despicable hut, a shed fit only for beasts, that we may know

---

162 Psalm 61:1
163 Psalm 61:1

that He it is "Who raiseth up the poor one from the dunghill," and "saveth men and beasts"—He Who said, "Unless, you be converted and become as this little child, you shall not enter into the kingdom of heaven."[164]

Would that we also might be found to be a Bethlehem of Judah, so that in us also He might deign to be born, and that we might deserve to hear: "To you who fear my name the sun of justice shall arise."[165] Perhaps this refers to what we said above, that we are to see Majesty amongst us, and that there is need of sanctification and preparation, for, according to the Psalmist, "Judea is become his sanctification"—that is, we are all cleansed and sanctified by confession. Bethlehem—as "House of bread"—seems to relate still more to the preparation for the feast. For how could *he* be ready to receive so great a guest who said, "In my house there is no bread"[166]? The man in the Gospel was likewise unprepared when he was obliged to rouse his friend in the middle of the night, and say: "My friend has come to me on a journey, and I have nothing to set before him."

The Prophet tells us that the just man's heart "is ready to hope in the Lord," and that "it is strengthened, and shall not be moved."[167] The heart, then, that is not strengthened is not ready. But we know from the same Prophet that "bread strengthens the heart of man."[168] He, therefore, who forgot

---

[164] Matthew 5:3
[165] Matthew 18:3
[166] Malachi 4:2
[167] Psalm 3:8
[168] Psalm 103:15

to eat his bread had not his heart ready, but had left it dry and lifeless. The just man, on the contrary, keeps his heart ready and unmoved, prepared to keep the Commandments of God. Like the Apostle, he forgets the things which are behind, and stretches forth himself to those that are before.[169] Thus you see there are some things which we must fly from, and about which a certain forgetfulness is desirable. There are others which should never be lost sight of. It is said of one man that he was unmindful of the Lord his Creator, of another that he kept Him ever before his eyes, having forgotten his people and his father's house. This last forgot the things that are seen and are upon the earth; the other those that are not seen and are heavenly. The good Christian forgets the things that are his own to remember those of Jesus Christ. Such a one is ready to see the majesty of God within him, while the negligent and forgetful Christian is very unprepared. He is not the house of bread in which our Saviour dwells. He is not the Manasses to whom Christ, Who rules Israel, appears, and Who as God "sits upon the cherubim," and to Whom the Psalmist exclaims, "Shine forth before Ephraim, Benjamin, and Manasses."[170]

I think that these three men represent all that are saved, and to whom another Prophet alludes as Noe, Daniel, and Job[171]; and that they also prefigure the three shepherds, to whom the angel announced "a great joy" at the birth of the "angel of the great council." Perhaps they represent also the

---

[169] Psalm 3:13
[170] Psalm 79:1–3
[171] Ezekiel 14:14

three Magi. In this sense, it may not seem unfitting to attribute to Ephraim, which name means "Fruitfulness," the offering of the incense, since to offer worthy incense in the odour of sweetness is the office of those whom God has appointed to go and bring forth fruit—that is, the prelates of the Church. And, as Benjamin means "Son of the right hand," he must give the gold—that is, the substance of this world—in order that the faithful people may be placed on the right hand at the Last Day, and deserve to hear from the Judge, "I was hungry, and you gave me to eat,"[172] and the rest. As for Manasses, if he would be one of whom "the Lord appears," let him offer the myrrh of mortification, and this, I think, is especially required in our sacred profession of the religious life.

We have digressed. Let us now return "to Bethlehem, and see this word that is come to pass, which the Lord hath showed to us."[173] It is the house of bread, and we have already said that "it is good for us to be there." For where the word of God is there will be no lack of the bread which strengthens the heart, as the Prophet says, "Strengthen thou me in thy words."[174] We also read, "Man liveth by every word that proceedeth from the mouth of God"; then he liveth in Christ, and Christ liveth in him. In his heart Christ is born, to him Christ appears—Christ, Who loves not the faltering, wavering heart, but the strong and steadfast heart. One who murmurs, who hesitates, who wavers in his purpose, who

---

[172]Matthew 25:35
[173]Luke 2:15
[174]Psalm 118:28

thinks of returning to what he has left, of relinquishing his vow, of changing his state of life, is no Bethlehem, no house of bread. Christ is not born in such a heart as this, where the fortitude of faith and the bread of life are wanting, for the Scripture says, "The just man liveth by faith,"[175] and Christ, the true life of the soul, dwells in our heart by faith. Besides, how could Christ be born in that heart, how could such a one attain salvation, when the sentence is so utterly true that "he only that perseveres to the end shall be saved"? How could the proud and vacillating heart belong to a follower of the Son of God whose spirit rests only "on him that is poor, and little, and of a contrite spirit, and that trembleth at his words"? For there can be no connection between eternity and such fickleness, between him who is and him who never remaineth in the same state.

But if we are strong, if we are constant in faith, if we are ready to receive our Lord, if we abound in bread, we owe it entirely to His bounty to whom we say daily, "Give us this day our daily bread," though we have need also to add, "forgive us our trespasses," for "if we say we have no sin we deceive ourselves, and the truth is not in us." He is Truth itself Who is born not merely in Bethlehem, but in Bethlehem of Judah, Jesus Christ, the Son of God. Let us, then, come in before His presence with praise, that we may be found both sanctified and prepared, and so may deserve to see Christ born in ourselves, His Bethlehem of Judah.

---

[175] Habakkuk 2:14

# IV

# ON OUR LORD'S NATIVITY

**I**

## The Fountains of the Saviour

The solemnity of our Lord's Nativity is indeed a great and glorious day, but a short one, and a short day calls for a short sermon.

No wonder if we make a short speech, since God the Father has made an abbreviated Word—*Verbum abbreviatum*. Would you know how long and how short is the Word He has made? This Word says, "I fill heaven and earth,"[176] yet, now that "the Word is made flesh," He is placed in a narrow manger. The Psalmist exclaimed, "From eternity and to eternity thou art God,"[177] yet, behold! He is a Child of a day. And why this? What necessity was there that the Lord of Majesty should so annihilate Himself, should thus humble Himself, thus abbreviate Himself, except to show that we should do in like manner? He now proclaims by example what He will one day preach in words—"Learn of Me, for I am meek and humble of heart"—and He does so that the Evangelist might be proved truthful when he said of this Word, "Jesus began to do and to teach."

I therefore earnestly beseech you not to allow so precious an example to be set before you in vain. Conform yourselves to it, and be ye renewed in the spirit of your mind. Aim at

---

[176] Jeremiah 23:24
[177] Psalm 89:2

humility; it is the foundation and the guardian of all virtues. Follow after it, for it alone can save your souls. What is more deplorable, what more hateful, what more grievously punishable than that, after seeing the God of heaven become a Little One, man should any longer endeavour to glorify himself upon earth? It is an intolerable insolence that when Majesty has annihilated itself, a worm of earth should inflate and puff itself up. It was to make reparation for this pride that He Who, in the form of God, was equal to the Father, "emptied himself, taking the form of a servant."[178] He emptied Himself—yes, of His majesty and His power, not of His mercy and His goodness, for the Apostle tells us "the goodness and kindness of our Saviour hath appeared."[179] His power had appeared in the creation of the world, His wisdom has ever been manifested in its government, but now in His humanity His goodness and mercy are more specially made known. He had shown His power to the Jews in signs and prodigies; therefore you will often find in the writings of the Old Law such expressions as "I am the Lord," "I am God." To the ancient philosophers, abounding in their own sense, he likewise made His majesty known, according to those words of the Apostle, "That which is known of God is manifest in them, for God hath manifested it to them."[180] The Jews were subdued by this same power; the philosophers, searchers into majesty, were overwhelmed by His glory. Power exacts subjection, majesty inspires awe, but neither oblige to imitation. Let thy goodness, O' Lord, now appear, that man,

---

[178] Philippians 2:7
[179] Titus 3:4
[180] Romans 1:19

who is created in Thy likeness, may be conformed to it; for power, majesty, and wisdom are not what we can imitate, or what it is expedient that we should copy. In the case of the angels Thy mercy was withheld from a portion only of them; afterwards the whole human race was overwhelmed by Thy judgment.

Let mercy extend her dominion, let her reach from end to end mightily, and dispose all things sweetly. In the past, O' Lord, Thou didst limit Thy mercy by judgment; come, we beseech Thee, now, flowing with compassion and overflowing with charity. What dost thou fear, O' man? Why dost thou tremble before the face of the Lord "because He cometh"? It is not to judge the earth that He comes, but to save it. Fly not, O' man, fear not; Jesus comes not in anger, He comes not to punish: He comes to seek thy salvation. And lest thou shouldst say even now, "I heard thy voice, and I hid myself,"[181] behold, He comes as an Infant, and without speech, for the voice of the wailing infant arouses compassion, not terror. If He is terrible to any, yet not to thee. He is become a Little One, His Virgin Mother swathes His tender limbs with bands, and dost thou still tremble with fear? By this weakness thou mayest know that He comes not to destroy, but to save; not to bind, but to unbind. If He shall take up the sword, it will be against thine enemies, and, as the Power and the Wisdom of God, He will trample on the necks of the proud and the mighty.

---

[181] Genesis 3:10

We have two enemies, sin and death—that is, the death of the soul and the death of the body. Jesus comes to conquer both, and to save us from both. Already He has vanquished sin in His own person by assuming a human nature free from the corruption of sin. For great violence was offered to sin, and it knew itself to be indeed subdued, when that nature which it gloried to have wholly infected and possessed was found in Christ perfectly free from its dominion. Henceforth Christ will pursue our enemies, and will seize them, and will not desist until they are overcome in us. His whole mortal life was a war against sin. He fought against it by word and example. But it was in His passion that He came upon the strong man armed, and bound him, and bore away his spoils.[182]

Jesus Christ also conquers our second enemy, death. He overcomes it first in Himself, when He rises from the dead, the first-fruits of them that sleep, and the first-born from the dead. Afterwards He will, in like manner, vanquish death in all of us when He shall raise our mortal bodies from the dust, and destroy this our last enemy. Thus, when He rose from the dead, Jesus was clothed in beauty, not wrapped in swaddling-clothes as at His birth. He that previously overflowed with mercy, "judging no man," girded Himself in His resurrection with the girdle of justice, and in so doing seemed in some degree to restrain His superabundant mercy in order to be

---

thenceforth prepared for the judgment which is to follow our future resurrection.

But Christ comes now, in His Nativity, as a Little One, with the prerogative of mercy, that His mercy, going before, may temper the justice of our future judgment. Although He comes as a Little One, the gifts He brings are not little, the treasures He bestows are not little. In the first place, He brings mercy, for the Apostle testifies: "According to his mercy he hath saved us." Neither was it only to those among whom He lived that He brought these benefits. Christ our Lord is a fountain that can never be exhausted. He is a fountain for us, too, wherein we may be washed from sin; as it is written, "who hath loved us, and washed us from our sins."[183] But water not only washes away our stains, it likewise quenches our thirst. This is the second use of the fountain, and the Wise Man says: "Justice shall give him the wholesome water of wisdom to drink."[184]

The water of wisdom is rightly called wholesome, for the wisdom of the flesh is death, and the wisdom of the world is the enemy of God. The only wholesome wisdom is the wisdom that is from God, and which, according to St. James's definition, "is first chaste, then peaceable."[185] The wisdom of the flesh is sensual, not chaste. The wisdom of the world is turbulent, not peaceable. But the wisdom that is of God is first chaste, not seeking the things that are her own, but those

---

[183] Revelation 1:5
[184] Ecclesiasticus 15:3
[185] James 3:17

that are Jesus Christ's; for, let no one do his own will, but consider what is the will of God. It is, then, peaceable, not abounding in her own sense, but rather yielding to the counsel or judgment of another.

The third use of water is for irrigation. This is specially needed by young plantations and seeds newly sown, lest they be either stunted in growth, or wither away through want of moisture. Let, then, everyone who wishes to sow the seed of good works seek the water of devotion, that, being fertilized by the fountain of grace, the source of a good life, he may not wither away, but make progress in continual freshness of spirit.

Let us now see if we can find a fourth fountain, and win back our paradise, to be beautified, like that of old, by the water from four fountains or springs. Because if we do not desire to have the earthly paradise restored to us, how shall we hope for the kingdom of heaven? "If I have spoken to you earthly things, and you believe not, how will you believe if I shall speak to you heavenly things?"[186] In order, therefore, that by the manifestation of things present the expectation of the future may be made sure, we have a paradise far better and more delightful than that of our first parents. Our paradise is Christ our Lord. In this paradise we have already found three fountains; the fourth is yet to be sought. We have the fountain of mercy for washing away the stains of our sins; we have the fountain of wisdom, giving the waters of discretion for allaying our spiritual thirst; and we have the fountain of grace

---

[186] John 3:12

and devotion for irrigating the plants of our good works. The fourth fountain seems to be the fervid waters of charity. Hence the Prophet exclaims: "My heart grew hot within me, and in my meditation a fire broke forth."[187] And elsewhere: "The zeal of thy house hath eaten me up."[188] So that the just man loves justice from the sweetness of devotion, and hates iniquity from the fervour of zeal. Was it not of these four fountains that Isaiah spoke: "You shall draw waters with joy from the Saviour's fountains"[189]? And that we may know this promise to be spoken of the present life, not of that to come, mark what follows: "In that day, praise ye the Lord, and call upon his name." Invocation belongs to the present time, as it is written: "Thou didst call upon me in the day of tribulation, and I heard thee."[190]

Of these four fountains, three seem to apply specially to each of the three chief needs of the faithful. The first—remission—is common to all, for we all "offend in many things,"[191] and we have need of the fountain of mercy for washing away the stains of our sins. "We have all sinned, and do need the glory of God,"[192] whether prelates, virgins, or married people.

All Christians likewise, both the penitent and the devout, must have recourse to the second fountain, that of wisdom,

---

[187] Psalm 38:4

[188] Psalm 68:10

[189] Isaiah 12:3

[190] Psalms 80:8

[191] James 3:2

[192] Romans 3:23

for all walk in the midst of snares, and require its guidance to enable them to decline from evil and do good.

All, again, must hasten to the fountain of grace and devotion, that they may receive the unction necessary for fructifying their works and labours of penance and abstinence, and to enable them to act always in a spirit of cheerfulness, for "God loveth the cheerful giver." This grace we ask in the Lord's Prayer under the name of our daily bread.

In all these points nothing else seems to be meant but that our good works are to be seasoned with the fervour of devotion and the spiritual sweetness of grace.

The fourth fountain of zeal seems more specially suited to those in authority.

These four fountains our Blessed Lord offers to us in His own person while we still live on earth. A fifth, which is the fountain of life, He promises to give us in the world to come. This is the water for which the holy Prophet thirsted: "My soul hath thirsted after the strong living God."[193]

Was it to signify the first four fountains that Christ was wounded in four places while still living on the Cross? while the fifth wound in His side was not inflicted till after He had expired. Jesus Christ offers us the first four fountains during our life. He opens the fifth fountain to us after our death, when He leads us into the possession of eternal life.

---

[193] Psalm 41:3

But see how, after treating of the mysteries of our Lord's Nativity, we have suddenly turned to the mystery of His Passion. Yet it is no wonder that we should seek in the Passion for the treasures that Christ brought us in His Nativity, since it was in His Passion that He poured out for us the price of our redemption.

## II

### The Three Comminglings

"Great are the works of the Lord,"[194] says the Psalmist. Great indeed are all God's works, but the mysteries which chiefly excite our wonder and admiration are naturally those which concern our eternal salvation. Hence the same Prophet sings: "The Lord hath done great things for us."[195] His munificent dealings with us are shown forth chiefly in our Creation, our present redemption, and our future glorification. O' Lord, how greatly art Thou exalted in all Thy works! Do Thou proclaim their excellence to Thy people, and let us not be silent concerning them.

There is a threefold commingling to be considered in these three mysteries, most manifestly heavenly, most evidently the effect of the omnipotence of God. In the first of these mysteries, that of our creation, "God made man from the slime of the earth, and breathed into his face the breath of

---

194 Psalm 110:2
195 Psalm 125:3

life."[196] What a wonderful Creator, Who unites and commingles things so opposite! At His beck the slime of the earth and the spirit, or breath of life, are united, and make one being. The earth of which He made man had been previously created when "in the beginning God created the heavens and the earth." But the origin of the spirit was special, not common. It was not infused into the mass of matter, but is specially breathed into each individual of the human race.

O' man, acknowledge your dignity! Recognize the glory of human nature! You have a body taken from this earth, for it was fitting that one who is the appointed lord of all visible creatures should bear a similarity to them. But you are at the same time more noble and more exalted than they; nor are they in any way to be compared to you. In you body and soul are closely united; the first is moulded and fashioned, the second is inspired. On which side lies the advantage? Which of the two is the gainer in this union? According to the wisdom of this world, where what is low and mean is associated with what is excellent, those who are in power lord it over their inferiors, and bend them to their will. The strong man tramples on him who is the weaker; the learned man ridicules one who is unlearned; the crafty one deceives the simple; the powerful man despises the weak. It is not thus, O' God, in Thy work, not thus in Thy commingling. It was not for such a purpose that Thou didst unite spirit with matter; what is exalted with what is lowly; a noble and excellent creature with the abject, worthless clay. Thou didst will the

------

[196] Genesis 2:7

soul to rule; at the same time who does not see what dignity and advantage it thus confers on the body? Would not the body without the soul be senseless matter? From the soul it derives its beauty, from the soul its growth, from the soul the brightness of the eye and the sound of the voice. All the senses are animated by the soul. By this union charity is commended to me. I read of charity in the very history of my own creation. Not only is charity proclaimed in its first page; it is imprinted within me by the gracious hand of my Maker.

Great indeed is this union of body and soul; would that it had remained firm and unbroken! But, alas! though it had been secured by the Divine seal—for God made man to His own image and likeness—the union was marred, for the seal was broken and the likeness defaced. The worst of thieves approached, stealthily damaged the yet fresh seal, and so sadly changed the Divine likeness that man is now compared to senseless beasts, and is become like unto them.

God made man just, and of this his likeness to God it is written: "The Lord our God is righteous, and there is no iniquity in him."[197] He made man just and truthful, as He Himself is justice and truth; nor could this union be broken while the integrity of the seal was preserved. But that forger came, and, while promising a better seal, broke, alas! that which had been stamped by the hand of God. "You shall be as gods," he said, "knowing good and evil."[198] O' malicious one! O' crafty spirit! Of what use to that man and woman could

---

197 Psalm 91:16
198 Genesis 3:5

the likeness of this knowledge be? Let them "be as gods "by all means, but let them be upright, truthful, like God, in Whom there is no sin. While this seal remained whole the union remained uninjured. Now we have a woeful experience of what we were persuaded to attempt by the devil's craft. The seal once broken, a bitter parting followed, a sad divorce. O' wicked wretch! where is your promise, "You shall not die"? Behold, we all die. There is no man living that shall not taste death. What, then, will become of us, O' Lord our God? Will no one repair Thy work? Will noone help to raise the fallen? None can remake but He Who first made. Therefore, "by reason of the misery of the needy, and the groans of the poor, now I will arise, saith the Lord. I will set him in safety: I will deal confidently in his regard."[199] The enemy shall not prevail over him, nor the son of iniquity have any power to hurt him. Behold, I now make a new mixture, upon which I set a deeper and stronger seal. I will give to fallen man Him Who was not *made* to My likeness, but Who *is* the very image and splendour of My glory and the figure of My substance; not made, but begotten before all ages.

The first mixture was compounded of two things, earth and spirit. The second is made up of three, that from this fact we may learn to contemplate the mystery of the Blessed Trinity—the Word Who was in the beginning with God, and was God; the soul, which was created out of nothing, and had no previous existence; and the flesh, taken from corrupted nature without any corruption, separated and singled out by

---

[199] Psalm 11:6

a Divine plan, as if it had not been a portion of mortal flesh; and these three are united together in one Person, our Lord and Saviour Jesus Christ. We have in these three a threefold exhibition of power. What was not was created; what had perished was recreated; and what was higher than all was made a little lower than the angels. Here are the three Gospel measures of meal which are, as it were, fermented, that they may become the bread of angels, in order that man may eat the bread which strengthens his heart. Happy Mary! blessed amongst women, in whose chaste womb that bread was prepared by the Holy Ghost Who came down upon thee! Yea, happy woman! who hid in these measures the leaven of thy own glorious faith; so that by faith thou didst conceive Him, by faith thou didst bring Him forth, and by thy faith those things were accomplished in thee which were spoken to thee by the Lord, and for believing which Elizabeth declared thee blessed.

And who need wonder when I say that the Word was united to human flesh through the faith of Mary, seeing that He received that same flesh from hers? There is nothing in the foregoing explanation opposed to our regarding the faith of Mary as a type of the kingdom of heaven; nor does it seem unfitting to compare her faith with the kingdom of heaven, since by that same faith its losses are repaired. This bond of union, this Trinity in Christ, no human power could wholly sever. The "prince of this world" had nothing in Him, the latchet of whose shoe the Baptist himself was unworthy to loose. Yet it was necessary that this triad should in a certain way be dissolved; otherwise, what is not dissolved cannot be reconstructed. Of what use are bread unbroken, a treasure hidden, wisdom concealed? Well might St. John weep when no one was found to open the book and break its seals. Whilst it remained closed, no man amongst us could attain to its Divine wisdom. O' Lamb of God! O' truly meek Lamb! do Thou open the book. Open out Thy pierced hands and feet, that the treasure of salvation and the plentiful redemption hidden in them may come forth. Break Thy bread to the hungry. Thou alone canst break it to them, Who alone couldst stand firm and unshaken when the union between Thy Divine and human natures appeared broken in Thy passion. In this breaking Thou still hadst power to lay down Thy life and to take it up again. In Thy mercy Thou didst to a certain degree destroy this temple, but didst not wholly dissolve it. Let the soul be separated from the body, the Word will preserve that flesh from corruption and bestow a full liberty on the soul, that it alone of all human souls may be free among the dead, and lead forth from the prison-house those who were bound, those sitting in darkness and in the shadow of death. Let this holy and Divine soul lay down its immaculate flesh, that by dying it may conquer death; but let it resume that flesh on the third day, that by rising again it may raise us all from death to life. This has been done, and let us rejoice in the accomplishment of the mystery. By that death, death is destroyed, and by the Resurrection of Jesus Christ from the dead we are regenerated in the hope of life.

But who shall say what is to take place in the third and future union? "Eye hath not seen, ear hath not heard, nor hath it entered into the heart of man to conceive what God hath prepared for them that love Him." The consummation of the union will be when Christ shall have restored and given back the kingdom to God and the Father.

To sum up, in the first mixture, where man is made and composed of body and soul, we saw charity recommended. In the second mixture or union, the Incarnation, humility shines pre-eminent in the infinite condescension of God in assuming our human nature, whereby He teaches us that it is by humility alone we can repair the wounds of charity.

In the first union it is no result of humility that the rational soul is united to an earthly body, for it is not by any deliberate act of its own. The soul is immediately breathed into it by God.

It is otherwise in the second union, where the Uncreated Spirit, Himself the Sovereign Good, humbly drew nigh to our nature, and of His own will and choice assumed an unsullied body.

From both we learn that charity and humility are deservedly followed by glorification, for without charity nothing can profit us, and without humility none shall be exalted. In humility, then, is laid up for us the perfection of the beatitude which we expect and long for. May we be so blest as to attain it!

# III

## On the Place, Time, and Other Circumstances

In the Nativity of our Blessed Lord there are two things to be considered, both exceedingly different, exceedingly wonderful. The Child Who is born is God, the Mother of whom He is born is a Virgin, and her child-bearing is without pain. To celebrate these new wonders a new light from heaven shines forth in the darkness of midnight. The angel announces tidings of great joy. A multitude of the heavenly army praise God and sing, "Glory to God on high, and peace on earth to men of good-will." The shepherds hasten to find the Word that has been announced to them. They proclaim it to others, and all that hear are filled with admiration. Mysteries such as these are signs of Divine power, not of human weakness. They are as the gold and silver vessels, from which, on account of the solemnity, even the poor are served at our Lord's Sacred Table.

The wise man says, "Consider diligently the things set before thee."[200] I may truly claim to myself the time and place of this Nativity, the weakness of His infantine body, the tears and cries of this sweet Little One, as well as the poverty and vigils of the shepherds to whom our Saviour's Nativity was first announced. These circumstances are truly mine; for me they were planned, before me they have been placed, and

---

[200] Proverbs 23:1

they are offered to me for my spiritual food, for my contemplation.

Christ was born in winter. He was born in the night. And are we to believe that His coming into the world in such an inclement season and in the darkness of night are mere casual events, matters simply fortuitous? From Whom come winter and summer, day and night? Other children that as yet have hardly begun to live do not choose the time of their birth; they have not the use of reason, nor liberty of choice, nor faculty of deliberation. But Christ, though man, was nevertheless God. He was in the beginning with God. He was God, the same of Whom He is the Power and the Wisdom, for He is "the Power and the Wisdom of God." Therefore, the Son of God, in Whose power it remained to do whatever He willed, when about to be born, chose His own time, and chose, too, what was most specially burdensome to a little child and to the son of a poor mother who had hardly sufficient linen wherewith to swathe Him and no cradle wherein to place Him. And though so great was His necessity, and He God, we hear no mention of a rich and warm coverlet for His Divine and royal members. The first Adam was clothed in a tunic of skins; the second Adam was swathed in rags. Such things are not according to the judgment of this world. Either Christ is deceived, or the world errs. But that the Divine Wisdom could be deceived is impossible. Justly, therefore, is the prudence of the flesh an enemy of God; for the prudence of the flesh is death, and the prudence of the world is folly. What follows? Christ, Who could not be deceived, chose what was painful and troublesome; therefore it is the best, the most profitable choice, that which is to be preferred to all others, and whoever teaches or persuades to the contrary is to be avoided as a tempter and deceiver.

Our Blessed Lord willed to be born in the obscurity of night. Where are they who so shamelessly and studiously display themselves and their actions in the blaze of day? Christ chose what He judged to be most salutary; they choose what He rejected. Which of the two is the more prudent choice? Whose judgment the more just? Whose sentence the more reasonable?

Christ is born in a stable, and lies in a manger. Yet is He not the same that said, "The earth is mine and the fullness thereof"? Why, then, need He choose a stable? Plainly that He might reprove the glory of the world, that He might condemn its empty pride. The Infant Jesus is silent. He does not extol Himself; He does not proclaim His own power and greatness, and behold, an angel announces His birth, a multitude of the heavenly host praise and glorify the new-born King. You that would follow Christ do in like manner imitate His example. Hide the gifts and graces you have received. Love to be unknown. Let the mouths of others praise you, but keep your own lips closed.

His tongue has not spoken, and, behold, everywhere He is proclaimed, preached, made known. These infantine members will not be silent; they have another kind of language: in all of them the judgment of the world is reproved, subverted, and set at naught. What man with intelligence, being free to choose, would not prefer a full-grown, robust body rather than that of an infant? O' Divine Wisdom! Thou art manifested by Thy preference for what was hidden and abject. O' truly Incarnate Wisdom, veiled in the flesh! This is nevertheless what was long ago prophesied by Isaiah: "The child will know how to refuse evil and choose good." The pleasures of the body are the evil which He refuses; affliction is the good He selects. And assuredly, He that makes His choice is a wise Child, a wise Infant. He is the eternal Word of God, for the Word was made flesh—infirm flesh, tender flesh, the feeble, helpless flesh of an Infant, incapable of its own nature of any good work, feeling a repugnance to labour and hardships. Truly the Word was made flesh, and in flesh dwelt amongst us.

When in the beginning the Word was with God, He dwelt in light inaccessible, and there was none that could bear that light. For who hath known the mind of the Lord, or who hath been His counsellor? The carnal man of His own nature perceives not those things which are of the Spirit of God; but now he can perceive them though still carnal, for the Word was made flesh. Since man, on account of the flesh, could understand nothing but what was of the flesh, behold, the Word was made flesh that man might be able even by the flesh to hear and understand the things of the Spirit. O' man, behold that wisdom which was heretofore hidden is shown forth to you! It is now drawn forth from its hiding-place, and is laid open to you, and it penetrates into the very perceptions of your nature.

I have already said that He preaches to you even in His Infancy, and says: "Fly from pleasure, for death follows swiftly when sensual pleasure enters. Do penance, for the kingdom of God is at hand." The Stable preaches this penance to us, the Manger proclaims it to us; this is the language which His Infant members speak; this is the Gospel He announces by His cries and tears. Christ weeps, but not as the rest of children—that is, not for the same cause. In other children it is from the suffering inflicted on their senses, in Christ the affections were the source of His sufferings. *They* suffer but do not act, for they have no power as yet to use their will. They weep from passion, Christ from compassion. They weep under the heavy yoke laid upon every child of Adam; Christ deplores the sins of the children of Adam, and that for which He now sheds streams of tears He will afterwards pour out torrents of blood.

O' hardness of my stony heart! Would that as our Lord has been made flesh, so He would make my heart a heart of flesh. It is what He promised by His prophet Ezechiel. "I will take away the stony heart out of their flesh, and will give them a heart of flesh."[201] The tears of Christ fill me with shame and sorrow. I was taking my pastime without in the streets, and in the secrecy of the King's chamber the sentence of death was passed upon me. His only-begotten Son heard this judgment, and, laying aside His royal diadem, He went forth, sprinkled ashes upon His head, clothed Himself in sackcloth, bared His feet, and mourned and wept over the

---

[201] Ezekiel 11:19

condemnation of His poor slave. I see Him suddenly go forth. I am amazed at the strangeness of the spectacle. I demand, and am told, the cause. What course am I to take? Shall I still indulge myself and deride His tears? Yea, if I am mad, if I am wanting in mind, I shall fail to follow Him, I shall not weep with Him that weeps. Behold, whence comes my shame, whence is my sorrow, whence my fear? From the consideration of the remedy I may estimate the gravity of the danger. I knew it not. I thought my self in health, and lo! the Son of the Virgin is sent, the Son of the Most High God is sent, and it is even ordained that He shall be put to death in order that by the balsam of His precious Blood my wounds may be healed.

Understand, O' man, the grievousness of those wounds for the healing of which it was necessary that Christ our Lord should be wounded. Had they not been wounds unto death, and to eternal death, the Son of God would never have died for their remedy. We have indeed reason to blush and be confounded at our negligence in respect to the Passion of Christ, beholding as we do so much compassion shown to us by such infinite Majesty. The Son of God compassionates man, and weeps over him; man allows Him to do it, and keeps up incessant laughter.

Thus, by considering the remedy, my sorrow and my fear are increased. If I carefully observe the injunctions of my Physician, they will afford me consolation. For, though I recognize the grievousness of the disease for the cure of which such severe remedies were needed, from the very fact of their existence I conjecture that my disease is not incurable. The wise Physician would not apply such costly remedies in a hopeless case, for the very reason that He is a wise Physician—yea, Wisdom itself. Neither would He apply such remedies to a case easily curable without them, still less in one where cure was impossible. This hope in our Divine Physician's power and goodness excites us to penance, and enkindles in us the most ardent desire of virtue. This is the same consolation that the visit and discourse of the angels gave to the shepherds in their midnight vigils. Woe to you rich, for you have your consolation here; you do not deserve to have that which is heavenly. How many men noble according to family rank; how many of the powerful and wise of this world, were at that hour stretched restfully on their soft beds, not one of them being found worthy to behold the new and glorious light, to share in the "great joy," to hear the angels sing, "Glory to God on high"!

This teaches us that those who are not engaged in some useful labour or employment are not worthy to be visited by angels, and that labour undertaken with a pure intention is pleasing to the citizens of heaven. Indeed, they have been known to hold converse, and such happy converse, with the poor and laborious. Is it not, moreover, God's own law that man should earn his support by his own labour and exertions?

Let me, then, earnestly beseech you to consider attentively how much God has done for your instruction and salvation, that a "word so living and efficacious" may not be found fruitless in you. It is a word "faithful and worthy of all acceptance"; it is an efficacious word, no mere verbal expression.

I, who have been speaking to you, am but a miserable man, yet do you suppose it would be a small affliction for me if I were to find that my words had failed to produce any good results in your hearts? With how much more justice, then, will the Lord of all Majesty be indignant if our negligence, our slowness, our hardness of heart, were to make void and vain His great and precious labour.

May He Who for our salvation vouchsafed to clothe Himself in the form of a servant avert this evil from us His servants—He Who is the only-begotten Son of God the Father, God blessed for ever and ever. Amen.

## IV

### On the Shepherds Finding Our Lord

Observe how great is this day's solemnity, for which the day itself is too short and the breadth of the whole earth is too circumscribed. This day encroaches on the night, it anticipates the natural dawn. It fills heaven and earth with its brightness. It fills heaven before it fills the earth. For the night was made light as the day, when in the bitter midnight a new light from heaven shone around the shepherds. And that we might know in what place the joys of this solemnity began to be celebrated, and that it had already been a feast for the angels, immediately there was present a multitude of the heavenly host, sounding forth the Divine praises; and they proclaimed that it should be a day of joy for the people also.

For this reason this night is considered solemn beyond all others, and is spent in psalms and hymns and spiritual canticles. And while we thus keep vigil, we may undoubtedly believe that the heavenly princes unite still in our canticles, and even anticipate our psalmody.

See how many altars glitter to-day with gold and jewels! Behold how the walls of churches are adorned with costly hangings! Think you, then, that the angels will turn in preference towards these things and depart from men in poverty? If so, why did they choose to appear to the shepherds rather than to the kings of the earth and the priests of the Temple? Why did this same Saviour, to Whom belong the gold and the silver, consecrate holy poverty in His own person? It cannot be without some special mysterious reason that the Saviour of the world is wrapped in swaddling-clothes and laid in a manger. Thy swaddling-clothes, O' Lord Jesus, are given as a sign of Thee; but they are a sign that shall be contradicted by many even to this day, "for many are called, but few are chosen"; therefore few are signed with the sign of salvation.

Here I recognize and acknowledge in all truth the "great High Priest Jesus, covered with filthy garments"[202] in His Passion, while He contended with the devil. I speak here to those who are versed in the Scriptures, and to whom the

---

[202] Zechariah 3:1–5

prophetical vision of Zachary is not unknown. There we find our Head exalted above our enemies from the very fact that His vesture is changed. Yes, He has put on the stole of beauty, and clothed Himself with light as with a garment. He has given us an example that we also should do as He has done. When the members, following their Head on High, shall form but one body, then they will sing in one spirit: "Thou hast cut my sackcloth and hast compassed me with gladness."[203]

The angel said: "You will find the Infant wrapped in swaddling-clothes and laid in a manger." And a little later the Evangelist goes on to say: "They came in haste, and they found Mary and Joseph, and the Infant lying in the manger."

How is it that the angel mentions only the Infant, since that was not all that the shepherds were to find? Is he recommending humility in the Person of the Sacred Infant? If so, why humility specially? Perhaps because his fellow-angels fell by pride, while by humility he stood firm. Or it may be that humility is thus proclaimed to be a heavenly virtue, because it is that most fittingly exercised towards the Divine Majesty. Humility, however, can never be found alone. It cannot exist as a single virtue, for God gives His grace to the humble. Wherefore the shepherds found Mary and Joseph with the Infant laid in the manger. As humility is the virtue specially exemplified in the infancy of our Saviour, so chastity appears in the Blessed Virgin, and justice is suitably pointed out by the just man Joseph, so named in the Gospel.

---

[203] Psalm 29:12

We all know that continence and purity are to be observed in regard to the flesh. Justice is the virtue by which we render to everyone what is his due, and it is necessary in our dealings with others. Humility reconciles us with God, makes us subject to Him, and renders us well pleasing in His sight, as the Blessed Virgin testifies. "He has had regard to the humility of his handmaid." So that by impurity we sin against ourselves; by injustice against our neighbour; by pride and self-exaltation against God. The unchaste man dishonours himself; the unjust man is burdensome to his neighbour; the proud man, as far as in him lies, dishonours God. God has said: "I will not give my glory to another." The proud soul says: "As you will not give it to me, I will usurp it." Consequently such a one cannot relish the distribution by the angel, of giving "glory to God, and on earth peace to men of good-will." The proud man does not worship God, but impiously and faithlessly lifts himself up against Him. What is piety but the worship of God? And who pays true homage to God but the man that is willingly subject to Him? As the eyes of the servant are on the hands of his master, so are the eyes of the just man ever directed towards the Lord his God.

Therefore, let Mary and Joseph and the Infant be always found in us, that we may live soberly and justly and piously in this world. For it is for this purpose that the grace of God our Saviour hath appeared instructing us; and it is by the exercise of the virtues we have mentioned that His glory will appear. The Apostle says: "The grace of God hath appeared to all men, instructing us that, denying impiety and worldly desires, we may live soberly and justly and piously in this world, expecting the blessed hope and coming of the glory of the great God.

In the Little One there hath appeared grace for our instruction, because He will yet be great, as the angel Gabriel foretold. And they whom He, as a Little One, shall have instructed in humility and meekness of heart, He will afterwards exalt and glorify, when He shall come as great and glorious, Jesus Christ our Lord for ever. Amen.

**V**

## On the Words, "Blessed Be the God and Father of our Lord Jesus Christ"

"Blessed be the God and Father of our Lord Jesus Christ, the Father of mercies and God of all consolations, who comforts us in all our tribulations."[204]

**B**lessed be He Who, in the exceeding charity wherewith He has loved us, has sent His beloved Son, in Whom He is well pleased; by Whom, being reconciled, we have peace with God; and Who is at once our Mediator and the pledge of our reconciliation. Under so powerful a Mediator there is no ground for doubt; under so merciful a Protector we have no cause for fear. But, you will say, what sort of a Mediator is He Who is born in a stable, laid in a manger, and wrapped in swaddling-clothes as other children, Who weeps as other children, and lies before us subject to all the needs of infancy?

---

[204] 1 Corinthians 1:3, 4

I answer, He is a Mediator great in all things that appertain to our peace. He seeks that peace not perfunctorily or carelessly, but sincerely and efficaciously.

An Infant He truly is, but the Word—an Infant whose very childhood speaks more powerfully than the most eloquent discourse. "Be comforted, be comforted, my people, saith the Lord your God,"[205] saith our Emmanuel, our God with us. The stable proclaims it, the manger proclaims it, His tears and His swathing-bands proclaim it. The stable declares that He is preparing to cure the man that fell among robbers; His manger tells us that He will minister food to him that was compared to beasts, and made like unto them. His tears and His swaddling-clothes cry out that He will wash and cleanse man's wounds. Christ needed not any of these things for Himself. All were for His elect. "They will reverence My Son," says the Father of mercies. Yes, they will indeed reverence Him; but who are they who will render this homage? Not the Jews, *to* whom He was sent, but the elect, *for* whose sake He was sent. We will reverence Him in His manger, we will reverence Him on His cross, we will reverence Him in His sepulchre. We will receive devoutly Him Who is a feeble Infant for our sakes, Who was pallid in death for us, and Who was buried for us. With the Magi we will devoutly adore Him, with holy Simeon we will embrace the Infant Saviour, and so we shall "receive thy mercy, O' God, in the midst of thy temple." Because this is He of Whom we read, "The mercy of the Lord is from eternity," for who is

---

205 Isaiah 40:1

co-eternal with the Father unless the Son and the Holy Ghost? And these Divine Persons are not so much merciful as mercy itself. The Father is mercy, and the Father, Son, and Holy Ghost are but one mercy, as they are one Essence, one Wisdom, one Deity, one Majesty.

But as God the Father is called the Father of Mercies, who does not see that He thus points out His Son by an appropriate name? Justly is He called the Father of Mercies, whose property it is to have mercy and to spare.

But some may object: How can it be His property to have mercy, since "his judgments are a great deep"[206]? It is not said that His ways are mercy only, but that they are mercy and truth.[207] He is not less just than merciful, and He is praised for mercy and judgment. It is true He will have mercy on whom He will have mercy, and whom He wills He will harden. Yet since His property is to have mercy, He draws from Himself the matter and cause for mercy; the cause for judgment He finds in us, for mercy seems far nearer to His heart than condemnation. "Is it my will," he says, "that a sinner should die, and not rather that he should be converted and live?" Justly, therefore, He is called the Father, not of judgment, but of mercy. And this not only because a father is readier to have mercy than to show indignation, but also because as a Father He has compassion on the children that fear Him, and because to have compassion is a property inherent in Him, for He is the cause and source of mercy.

---

[206] Psalm 35:7
[207] Psalm 24:10

But if on this account God is the Father of mercy, why is He called the Father of *mercies*? God once said: "These two things have I heard, that power belongeth to God, and mercy to thee, O' Lord."[208] Moreover, the Apostle commends to us this same mercy as manifold, calling God the Father not of one mercy, but of "mercies"; not of one consolation, but of "all consolation"; Who comforts us not in this tribulation or that, but in all our tribulations. The mercies of the Lord are many, says the Prophet. They are many; for many are the tribulations of the just, and out of them all the Lord will deliver them. The Son of God is One, the Word of God is one; but our misery is manifold, and demands not only great mercy, but a multitude of mercies.

Perhaps, on account of the two substances, spirit and matter, which make up our human nature, and each of which is subject to many troubles, man's misery may be said to be multiplied, as well in body as in soul. In truth, our tribulations, both of body and soul, are multiplied, but from the necessities of both we are delivered by Him Who saves the whole man. Since, then, the One and Only Son of God is now come for the salvation of our souls—that is, to take away the sins of the world—and His second coming will be to raise up our bodies and make them conformable to the body of His glory, it is not surprising if we confess in Him this twofold mercy and bless Him as Father of mercies.

---

When the Son of God assumed our nature, and took both a body and a soul, He said not once only, "Be comforted," but, as you saw above, the consolation is repeated: "Be comforted, be comforted, O' my people, saith the Lord your God."[209] This repetition is to assure us that He Who disdained not to receive both a body and a soul will work out the salvation of both in us. But as He will not save all indiscriminately, in whom will He effect this salvation? In "his people" certainly, for it is said, "he will save his people from their sins." Likewise, hereafter, He will not make all bodies like to the "body of his glory," but only the bodies of the humble. He will comfort His people. He will save a humble people; but the proud He will bring low.

Would you know who are His people? "To thee," says the man according to God's own heart—"to thee the poor man is left." Jesus Himself says in the Gospel, "Woe to you rich, for you have now your consolation." God grant, dearly beloved, that we may always be found among God's people, to whom He does not say "Woe"—the people whose comforter is the Lord their God.

Who will care to offer consolation to those who already abound in worldly comforts? The silent Infancy of Christ will not console the talkative; the tears of Christ will be no comfort to one given up to worldly enjoyments; the swaddling-clothes of Christ will offer no attraction to those

---

[209] Isaiah 40:1

who are clad in soft garments; the stable and the crib will only repel the lovers of the first places in the synagogues.

This universal consolation of Christ will, perchance, be found to descend preferably upon those who await their Lord in peaceful silence; on those who are in affliction; on those who are poor and detached from the world. Let such as these hear how the very angels console them. It is to these, not to others, that the holy angels whisper consolation. It is to the shepherds, watching and keeping the night watches over their flocks, that the joy of the new light is announced. To them it is revealed that the Saviour is born. Yes, to the poor, to the hard-working, not to the rich, who have their consolation here below. It is to the poor that the light of a glorious day has shone forth amid their vigils, and the night shall be light as the day—yea, it is converted into day. "This day," says the angel, not *this night*, "is born to you a Saviour." The night is truly past, the day is at hand—a day of days, the day of the salvation of our God, Jesus Christ our Lord, Who is God blessed above all for evermore. Amen.

# V

# ON THE CIRCUMCISION

"After eight days were accomplished that the child should be circumcised, his name was called Jesus."[210]

**In** these few words we have heard the great sacrament of piety set forth. We have heard the abbreviated Word which the Lord has revealed upon the earth. For He was "abbreviated" in taking flesh, and is still further "abbreviated" in receiving the circumcision of the flesh. In clothing Himself with human nature, the Son of God was made a little lower than the angels; but now that He does not disdain to submit to the remedy of human corruption, He is clearly made much lower than they. Here is a great teaching of faith, a manifest example of humility.

To what end could circumcision serve Him, Who had neither contracted sin nor committed it? That He had not committed sin His age is a proof; that He had not contracted it is manifest from the Divinity of His Father and the integrity of His Mother. He is the High Priest Who "neither for father nor mother shall be defiled"; and these words of Scripture are rather a prophecy of Him than a command of the law. His Father is from eternity, and He Himself is God, upon Whom no sin can fall. His Mother is of time, but she is a Virgin; and incorruption could not yield corruption.

Notwithstanding all this, the Child, the Lamb without spot, is circumcised. Though He stood in no need of circumcision, He willed to submit to that humiliating ceremony. Though He was without wounds, He shrank not

---

[210] Luke 2:21

from binding up our wounds. This is not the way the impious act; it is not thus with the perversity of human pride. We glory in our wounds, and blush to have them bound up and healed; while He Whom no man can convince of sin is the remedy of sin, and, without any necessity on His own part, receives both its shame and its punishment, and submits to the sacrificial knife. We, on the contrary, though shameless in sins, blush to do penance for them, and this is the excess of folly. It is a misery to be prone to sins; it is a greater one to be ashamed of their remedy. He that "did no sin" disdained not to be reputed a sinner; *we* are willing to be sinners, but not to be reputed as such.

In this mystery we see Him Who is in health taking the medicine intended for the sick, submitting to the remedy which they refuse.

"And after eight days were accomplished that the child should be circumcised, his name was called Jesus."

O' great and wonderful sacrament! The Child was circumcised and called Jesus. What connection does the Evangelist wish to show between these two facts? Circumcision would seem to belong more properly to the saved than to the Saviour. It was more befitting Him Who was the great High Priest to perform the rite to others than to submit to it Himself. He allowed it to be administered to Him in order to teach us that He is the Mediator between God and man, Who by His Nativity united His Divinity to our human nature—what is highest to what is lowliest.

He was born of a woman, but of a woman in whom the flower of virginity flourished together with the fruit of fecundity. He was wrapped in swaddling-clothes, but He was honoured with the praises of the angelic host. He lay in an obscure manger, but a radiant star from heaven pointed Him out. In like manner, by undergoing the rite of circumcision, He gave further proof of His human nature, but the adorable name of Jesus which He then received is above every other name, and declares the glory of His majesty. He was circumcised as a true son of Abraham; as Son of God He is called Jesus. This my Jesus bears not, as others do, an empty name; it is not in Him a shadow of greatness, but the reality. Heaven assigned it to Him, for the Evangelist testifies that the angel gave it to Him. And mark the depth of the mystery. It was *after* His birth that He was called by men Jesus, the name which had been given Him by the angel *before* His birth. For He is truly the Saviour of both angels and men; of men by His Incarnation, of angels from the beginning of creation. Before His birth the angels, who possessed the secrets of God, were allowed to know and utter the sacred name of salvation, but till this day of the Circumcision we knew it not. On this day it was first given me to pronounce confidently the blessed name of my Jesus, the name of my eternal salvation. Can we now doubt or hesitate to proclaim that He Who has condescended to dwell amongst us will work out the salvation of all those who are His own?

Circumcision is necessary for us also, in order that we may receive this name of salvation——a circumcision not according to the letter, but one in spirit and in truth. After the fall of our first parents human nature was wholly infected with the venom of sin. While the human race was yet, as it were, in infancy as to faith and love, man received a commandment suited to his imperfect condition. When he had grown to the age of the more perfect man he received the command of baptism, by which the entire man is circumcised. In like manner our Saviour was circumcised in His infancy, and, in His perfect manhood, was pleased to be crucified and to endure a penalty which caused every member of His body and every power of His soul to suffer. What, then, is our moral circumcision, if not what the Apostle recommends, "Having food and raiment, with these we are content"[211]? The circumcision of the religious life is voluntary poverty, the labours of penance, and the observance of regular discipline.

We should, therefore, admit nothing into the soul which we fear would not be acceptable to Him Whose Name is a name of salvation.

---

[211] 1 Timothy 6:8

# VI

# ON THE HOLY NAME OF JESUS AND OTHER SCRIPTURAL TITLES OF OUR LORD

"After eight days were accomplished that the child should be circumcised, his name was called Jesus."[212]

The eighth day is always the crowning day of the Church's greater festivals, and completes the celebration of the principal solemnities of the year. It is, as it were, linked with the first or opening day of the octave, just as our Lord in His Sermon on the Mount connected the eighth beatitude with the first by the promise of the kingdom of heaven.

When the Child that is born to us was circumcised He was called the Saviour, for it was then that He began the work of our salvation by shedding His precious blood for us. No Christian can now ask why Christ willed to be circumcised. For us He was born, for us He was circumcised, for us He suffered and died. Nothing of all this was for Himself, but all for His elect. He was not circumcised for His own sins, but for ours. The name He was called by the angel before His birth was His name from all eternity. This name of Saviour was His natural right; it was born with Him, not imposed by either angel or man. The illustrious Prophet Isaiah, predicting the birth of this Divine Child, calls Him by many great titles, but he seems to have been silent on this one name which the angel foretold, and to which the Evangelist bears testimony. Isaiah, like Abraham, exulted that he might see Christ's day; he, too, saw it and was glad. Rejoicing and praising God, he says: "A child is born to us, a son is given to us, and the government is upon his shoulder: and his name shall be called Wonderful, Counsellor, God the Mighty, the Father of the

---

[212] Luke 2:21

world to come, the Prince of Peace."[213] These are indeed great names, but where is *the* name which is above all names, the name of Jesus at which every knee should bow? Perhaps we may find that one name expressed, or poured out in all, for it is the same that was spoken of by the Spouse in the canticle of love, "Thy name is as oil poured out." Therefore, from and in all these names and titles we have but the one name of Jesus. His office of Saviour includes all. If one had been wanting, He could neither have been called nor have been the Saviour.

Has not each one of us found by experience that He has been Wonderful in the conversion and change of our wills? For is it not the beginning of salvation when we loathe what we formerly loved, grieve over what we once delighted in, embrace what we had feared, follow after that which we had fled from, desire what we had contemned? He that has wrought such wonders in us is assuredly Wonderful.

Jesus shows Himself to be the Counsellor by directing us in the choice of penance and of a well-ordered life, lest our zeal be without knowledge and our goodwill without prudence.

It was likewise necessary that we should experience Him to be God the Mighty. God in the remission of our past sins, for none but God can forgive sin, and Mighty when enabling us to fight victoriously those sinful passions which are ever

---

[213] Isaiah 9:6

warring in us, and which are liable to render our last state worse than the first.

Does anything still seem wanting to the office of Saviour? Yea, truly, the chief thing would be lacking were He not also the Father of the world to come, so that we who are engendered in this world unto death may by Him be raised up to a glorious immortality.

A further title and quality is required—that of the Prince of Peace Who has reconciled us to His Father, to Whom He is to give back the kingdom. Otherwise, as children of perdition, we might have risen again to punishment instead of reward.

The government, which is upon His shoulder, shall be magnified by the number of the saved, that He may be truly called the Saviour; that there may be no end of peace; and that we may know our salvation to be a true salvation which leaves no fear of failure.

O' blessed Name! O' sacred Oil! how widely hast thou been spread, how profusely poured out! Whence did this oil come? It came from heaven to Judea, and thence was diffused over the whole earth, to its uttermost bounds. The Church cries out, "Thy name is oil poured out." Poured out, indeed, to overflowing, since it is spread abroad, not only over the heavens and earth, but its influence reaches even to hell; so that "in the name of Jesus every knee shall bow, of those that are in heaven, on earth, and under the earth; and every tongue

shall confess"[214] and say, "Thy name is as oil poured out."
Behold the name of Christ and the name of Jesus were both
communicated to the angels and poured out upon men. I am,
then, made a participator in this salutary and life-giving name.
I am a shareholder in His inheritance. I am a Christian. I am a
brother of Christ. If a brother, then an heir also of God and
co-heir with Christ.

And what wonder that the name of the Divine Spouse is
poured out? In His passion He emptied Himself, taking the
form of a servant. By this pouring out the plenitude of His
divinity is diffused or spread abroad upon the earth, and of
His plenitude all shall receive; and when refreshed with the
life-giving perfume of this mystic oil they will exclaim, "Thy
name is as oil poured out."

But why is this name compared to oil? There is
undoubtedly a similitude between the name of the Spouse and
oil, and not without reason has the Holy Ghost drawn a
comparison between them. Oil gives light, nourishes and
strengthens the body, and alleviates pain. Hence it is light,
food, and medicine. All these qualities may be recognized in
the holy name of Jesus. It shines and gives light when
preached, it feeds and strengthens by its remembrance, it
alleviates sorrow and anoints the wounds of the soul by its
invocation. Let us consider these three qualities singly.

How was it that the light of faith shone forth so suddenly
over the whole earth, if not by the preaching of the blessed

---

name of Jesus? Is it not by the light of this name that God has called us "into his marvellous light,"[215] so that, being enlightened by it, we shall see light as the Apostle declares, "For you were heretofore darkness, but now light in the Lord."[216] The Apostle was commanded to carry this name before kings and nations, and the children of Israel. He carried it as a brilliant torch, and by it enlightened the nations sitting in darkness, so that he could exclaim: "The night is past, and the day, is at hand. Let us therefore cast off the works of darkness, and put on the armour of light. Let us walk honestly as in the day."[217] He lifted the light on high, and announced everywhere the name of Jesus and Him crucified. How brilliantly, too, did this light shine forth and attract the gaze of all when from the mouth of Peter the sacred name gave strength to the feet of the lame man at the Beautiful Gate of the Temple! Was he not diffusing this light when he said to this man, "In the name of Jesus Christ of Nazareth arise and walk"?[218] And to how many did he not restore sight, and health, and faith, by the power of this same name.

But the name of Jesus is not only light, it is likewise food. Are you not strengthened and consoled as often as you call it to mind? There is no thought that so replenishes and fills the soul with sweetness and spiritual joy; no exercise so efficaciously recruits and refreshes the wearied spirit, and even the senses; so repairs the inward strength, gives vigour

---

[215] 1 Peter 2:9
[216] Ephesians 5:8
[217] Romans 13:12
[218] Acts 3:6

to virtue, and cherishes pure affections, as the frequent invocation of the name of Jesus. All food of the soul is unsavoury to me if this oil be not poured upon it; it is insipid to me if not seasoned with this name. If you write, it does not relish if I read not there the name of Jesus. If you dispute or instruct, it does not satisfy me if I hear not the sweet sound of the name of Jesus. Jesus is honey to the mouth, music to the ear, jubilee to the heart.

The name of Jesus is, moreover, a sovereign medicine. If there be anyone overwhelmed with sorrow, let Jesus come into his heart, and thence to his lips, and behold, at the rising light of this sacred name all darkness and clouds will be dispersed, peace and joy will return, and the serenity of his mind will be restored. If there be anyone stained with crime, and driven headlong by despair to the pit of destruction, let him call upon this life-giving name, and he will speedily be restored to hope and salvation. Is there anyone amongst you in hardness of heart, in sloth, or tepidity, in bitterness of mind, if he will but invoke the name of Jesus his heart will be softened, and tears of contrition will flow gently and abundantly. In dangers and distress, in fears and anxieties, let him call on this name of power, and his confidence will return, his peace of mind will be restored. Doubts and embarrassments will be dispelled and give, place to certainty. There is no ill of life, no adversity or misfortune, in which this adorable name will not bring help and fortitude. It is a remedy whose virtue our dear Saviour invites us to test. "Call upon me in the day of trouble: I will deliver thee, and thou shalt glorify me."[219]

Nothing so efficaciously bridles anger and subdues the fire of all unruly passions as this holy name. When I pronounce the name of Jesus, I represent to myself a man meek and humble of heart, benevolent, chaste, merciful, a man endowed with all sanctity, all graces, all virtues, and I call to mind that this man is Divine, is the Almighty God, Who heals me by His example and strengthens me by His power. All manner of good things come to my mind when the sacred name of Jesus sounds in my ear. I will, therefore, make to myself a sweet and sovereign ointment from the virtues of His humanity and the Omnipotence of His Divinity. It shall be to me a healing balsam, the like to which no physician was ever able to compound. And this electuary, my soul, thou hast laid up in the little vessel of the name of Jesus.

Let, then, this name of power be ever in my heart, that all my thoughts, desires, and actions may be directed by Jesus and unto Jesus. To this He Himself urges me: "Place me as a seal upon thy heart, as a seal upon thy arm."

---

[219] Psalm 49:15

# VII

# ON THE EPIPHANY

# I

## On "The Goodness and Kindness of our Saviour hath Appeared"

"The goodness and kindness of God our Saviour hath
"appeared."[220]

Thanks be to God, through Whose mercy in this our pilgrimage, in this our banishment, in this our state of misery, unto us consolation also has greatly abounded. For this reason we have taken care often to admonish you that this our distance from our true country should not be long absent from our mind, and that we should be found ever hastening onwards to our heavenly inheritance. He that knows not desolation cannot appreciate consolation, and whosoever is ignorant that consolation is necessary shows plainly that he is not in God's favour.

Hence it is that men engrossed in the turmoil of worldly pursuits are unconscious of their misery, and neglect to hope for mercy. But to you it may be fitly said, "Taste and see that the Lord is sweet"[221]; to you the same Prophet says, "He will show forth to his people the power of his works."[222]

Therefore He willed to descend upon the earth, not only to be better known thereon, not merely to be born for

---

[220] Titus 3:4
[221] Psalm 33:9
[222] Psalm 110:6

us, but also to be acknowledged as our Saviour. This recognition is celebrated and proclaimed in to-day's solemnity, the Epiphany or day of manifestation.

To-day the Magi came from the East, seeking the risen Sun of justice, Him of Whom we read, "Behold a man, the Orient is his name."[223] To-day the Magi adored the new-born Child of the Virgin, following the guidance of the newly risen star. And have we not here a great cause for consolation? God spoke. They answered, not by their words, but by their works.

What are you doing, O' Magi? Do you adore a little Babe, in a wretched hovel, wrapped in miserable rags? Can this Child be truly God? God is in His holy Temple. God's seat is in the highest heaven, and do you seek Him in a poor stable, in the lap of a maiden-Mother? What are you doing? Do you offer Him gold? Is He, then, a King? If so, where is His palace? where His throne? where the retainers of His regal court? Is a stable His palace? a manger His throne? Are Mary and Joseph the sole occupants of His audience-chamber? Are you become foolish, O' Wise Men, that you can adore a Child, despicable alike for His age and for the poverty of His surroundings? Yes, these Wise Men have become fools that they may be wise. They are foretaught by the Holy Spirit, who afterwards breathed on the Apostle, when he said: "If any man among you seem to be wise, ... let him become a fool that he may be wise." Because, since the world could not through wisdom know God in His wisdom, it pleases God through the

---

[223] Zechariah 6:12

foolishness of preaching, as St. Paul calls it, to save those who believe.

Was it not to be feared that these men, beholding such signs of poverty, would be scandalized and believe themselves deluded? They expect to find the King in the royal city, but they are directed to little Bethlehem, "the least among the thousands of Judah." They enter the stable, they find the Babe in swaddling-clothes. The repulsiveness of the place deters them not, the swathing-bands offend them not, the Child at His Mother's breast shocks not their faith; they fall down and worship Him as their King, they adore Him as their God. And immediately, we may believe, He Who had led them thither Himself instructs them. He Who had spoken outwardly by the star now teaches them secretly in their hearts. This day is therefore made doubly glorious and sacred by the new manifestation of our Lord and by the devout adoration of the Magi.

But this is not the only manifestation celebrated on this day; there is a second, which, as we have learnt from our fathers in the faith, occurred on this same day, though after an interval of several years.

When our Blessed Lord, Who according to His Divinity "is always the selfsame and his years cannot fail," had completed the thirtieth year of His mortal life, He came amongst the crowds of the people to be baptized by John. He came as one of them, as a sinner, though He was without sin. Who would then have believed Him to be the Son of God? Who would have thought Him the Lord of Majesty? Thou art indeed exceedingly humbled, O' Lord. Thou art hidden amongst the lowest of the people, but Thou canst not hide Thyself from John, from him who, yet unborn, recognized Thee in Thy Mother's womb. Then his prophetic eye pierced through the double concealment; but as he was unable to cry out to the people, he made known his great joy to his mother. What will he *now* do? The Evangelist tells us. "John saw Jesus coming to him, and he saith: Behold the Lamb of God, behold him who taketh away the sin of the world." The true Lamb, the truly humble One, the truly meek One. Behold! this is He Who is to be the purification of our crimes.

Notwithstanding this noble testimony, Jesus wishes to be baptized by John. John trembles, and what wonder? What marvel that he, a mere man, shudders and dares not touch the sacred head of his Lord and God, that head adorable to the angels, venerable to the powers, terrible to the principalities?

O' Lord Jesus, wouldst Thou be baptized? But why? What need hast Thou of baptism? Do the healthy need medicine, or do those that are clean require to be purified? What has sin to do with Thee, that baptism should be necessary for Thee? Is it for the sin of Thy Father? But Thy Father is God, and who does not know that God cannot have sin? and Thou art equal to Him, God of God and Light of Light. Is it for Thy Mother's sin? But she is a Virgin conceived without sin, and in Thy birth she preserved her virginal integrity. What blemish, then, can be found in the Lamb without spot?

"I ought to be baptized by thee," says John, "and comest thou to me?" The humility of each is great, but may not be compared. How could man fail to humble himself before a humble God? "Suffer it to be so now," Jesus says, "for so it behoveth us to fulfil all justice."[224] John therefore consented and obeyed. He baptized the Lamb of God, and by their contact with our Lord the waters were cleansed. We were purified, not He; and the necessity of our being cleansed was prefigured in the purifying of the waters.

Lest, however, we should discredit the testimony of John—for he is a man, and liable to error, a relative, too, of Him to Whom he bears witness—a greater testimony is added to that of John—the Dove descends upon Christ. The dove is a fitting symbol to point out the Lamb of God. The lamb and the dove are equally the chosen emblems of perfect innocence, perfect gentleness, perfect simplicity; both are incapable of inflicting injury or practising deception.

That no one may suppose the appearance of the Dove to have been fortuitous, the testimony of God the Father is also added. "This is my beloved Son, in whom I am well pleased."[225] This is He Who later said of Himself, "I always do the things that please him."[226]

O' Lord Jesus, now at length speak to us, we entreat Thee. Too long—yea, greatly too long—Thou hast been silent and remained in obscurity. Now Thy Eternal Father's public recognition leaves Thee free to speak. How long shall the Power of God and the Wisdom of God remain hidden and

---

[224] Matthew 3:15
[225] Matthew 3:15
[226] John 8:29

unknown among the crowd? How long, O' noble King, O' King of Heaven, wilt Thou suffer Thyself to be called and be reputed the son of a carpenter?

O' humility! O' virtue of Christ! how terribly dost Thou confound our pride and vanity! I have, or, rather, I seem to myself to possess, some trifling knowledge, yet I cannot hold my tongue, but must shamelessly and recklessly thrust myself into notice only to make a display of what is rather my ignorance. I am ever prompt to speak, ready to impart my supposed knowledge, yet slow to accept information. Did, then, Christ fear vainglory even after His long silence and concealment? Why should He fear the glory of men Who is the true glory of the Father? He feared it not Himself, but for us, for whom it was very much to be feared, and thus He already warned and instructed us by His example what He would afterwards inculcate in word: "Learn of me, because I am meek and humble of heart."[227]

Concerning the infancy of our Blessed Lord the Gospel gives us some information, but of the years intervening between it and His public life it tells us absolutely nothing. Now, however, that His Heavenly Father has openly pointed Him out, He can no longer remain concealed.

The third mystery celebrated on this day is the marriage feast of Cana. As in His first manifestation He willed to appear in the company of His Blessed Mother, so now at the third we also find her present. Our Lord had been "invited and his

---

[227] Matthew 11:29

disciples to the marriage."[228] The wine failed. He had compassion on the confusion of the newly-married couple, and at the prayer of His Mother He vouchsafed to change water into wine. "This beginning of says St. John miracles did Jesus in Cana of Galilee,"[229]

In His first manifestation He was made known as truly man in the arms of His Mother; in the second as truly Son of God, from the testimony of His Eternal Father; in the third He is proved to be truly God, at Whose command Nature's laws are reversed. These three mysteries commemorated on this day are so many proofs to confirm our faith, so many promises to strengthen our hope, so many incentives to inflame our love.

## II

### "Go forth, ye Daughters of Jerusalem"

"Go forth, ye daughters of Zion, and see King Solomon in the diadem wherewith his mother crowned him."[230]

**O**f the three manifestations of our Lord, which all took place on this day, though not all at one time, the first is the most wonderful, though the second and third also greatly deserve our study and contemplation. The change of water into wine is an amazing miracle; the testimony of John, the descent of

---

[228] John 2:2, 3
[229] John 2:11
[230] Canticles 3:11

the Dove, the declaration of the Eternal Father, fill us with admiration; but the faith of the Magi in recognizing Christ under His disguise is indeed surpassingly wonderful.

By their adoration and their offering of incense they confess Jesus to be God. By their gold they show Him to be King as well as God. By their myrrh they acknowledge that His death, the sacrament of piety, had been revealed to them.

The Magi adore and offer gifts to an Infant in His Mother's arms. But where, O' Magi, is the purple of royalty? Do you not see the poor rags in which He is wrapped? If He is a King, where is His diadem? But you do see Him in the diadem with which His Mother crowned Him—His sacred body, of which He will say at His Resurrection: "Thou hast cut my sackcloth, and hast compassed me with gladness."[231]

"Go forth, ye daughters of Zion, and see King Solomon in the diadem wherewith his mother crowned him." Go forth, ye angelic hosts, ye citizens of the heavenly Jerusalem. Behold your King, but in *our* crown, in the diadem wherewith His Mother hath crowned Him; in the sacred humanity He has taken from us. Until now you have been deprived of these delights; up to this time you have not enjoyed this attractive sight. You have possessed Him in His Majesty, but not till this day have you seen Him in His humiliation. "Go forth, then, and see King Solomon."

Yet the angels need not our exhortation. This is He on Whom they ever desire to look. The more fully they know

---

His greatness, the more precious and lovable do they find His lowliness. And though His abasement is for us a greater source of joy, because it is for us He was born and to us He was given, nevertheless they have been beforehand with us, and have encouraged us to rejoice. The angel Gabriel proved this when he announced "a great joy"[232] to the shepherds. "And there was with the angel a multitude of the heavenly army."

Therefore it is to you, worldly souls, that we must direct these words "daughters of Zion"; to you, weak, delicate souls, daughters, not sons, in whom there is no fortitude, no manly courage. "Go forth, daughters of Zion." Go forth from the carnal mind to the understanding mind, from the servitude of the flesh to the liberty of the spirit. Go forth from your country, your kindred, your father's house, "and see King Solomon"; if you refuse, you may not safely meet Him in judgment. He is Solomon—that is, peaceful—in His dealings with us during our exile; He will be terrible in judgment; in His kingdom, as our reward, He will be our Beloved. In exile He is meek and amiable; in judgment just and terrible; in His kingdom glorious and wonderful. "Go forth," then, that you may see Him, for everywhere He is King. Although His kingdom is not of this world, He is nevertheless King in this world. When asked by Pilate, "Art thou a King?"[233] He replied: "For this was I born, and for this came I into this world." Here, then, He is the regulator of morals; in

<hr>

232 Luke 2:13
233 John 18:37

judgment He will be the discriminator of merits, in His kingdom the dispenser of rewards.

"Go forth, daughters of Zion, and see King Solomon in the diadem wherewith his mother hath crowned him," a crown of poverty, a crown of misery. Because, as He has been crowned on earth by His false mother—the Jewish Synagogue—with a crown of thorns, a crown of suffering, therefore should He be crowned by His children and servants with a crown of justice. For when He shall come to judge with the ancients of the people, the angels will go forth and gather all scandals out of His kingdom. Then all the earth shall fight for Him against the wicked and unwise. But the Father is now crowning Him with glory, as we read in the psalm, "Thou hast crowned him with glory and honour."[234]

Till then, behold Him, ye daughters of Zion, wearing the crown wherewith His mother hath crowned Him. Take up the humble crown of your King, become a Little One for your sake. Adore His humility, like the Magi whose faith and devotion are this day proposed for your imitation. To whom shall we compare these men? To whom shall we liken them? If we consider the faith of the penitent thief and the confession of the Centurion, the faith of the Magi seems to surpass theirs; inasmuch as the thief and Centurion had had the testimony of many miracles, our Lord's fame had been spread far and wide, He had been acknowledged and adored by many.

---

[234] Psalm 8:6

The good thief cried out from his cross, "Lord, remember me when thou comest into thy kingdom." His faith taught him that it was by His torments Christ was to enter into His kingdom. The Centurion's faith revealed to him the divinity of our Lord. When he heard Him cry out with a loud voice in the very act of expiring, he exclaimed, "Truly this man was the Son of God."

Oh, how wonderfully keen is the eye of faith! It knows the Son of God hanging on the cross, pierced with nails; it recognizes Him even in death, and here, in Bethlehem, with the Magi, it believes and confesses Him to be God, though a helpless Infant in the manger. What the others confessed by their words the Magi declared by their gifts. The thief believes Him a King; the Centurion, both man and the Son of God; the Magi acknowledge all three titles by their gold, their frankincense, and their myrrh.

I beseech you, therefore, dearly beloved, to draw profit from the immense charity which the God of Majesty has shown you; from the humility which He accepted; and from the loving kindness which has been made apparent to you through Christ's humility. Let us give thanks to our merciful Mediator and Redeemer, by Whom the good-will of God the Father has been made known to us. For we have now so known His mind that we may truly say: "We so run not as at an uncertainty."[235] For in truth the Father has given outward

---

235 1 Corinthians 9:26

expression to His love for us by sending into this world His only-begotten Son, our Lord and Saviour Jesus Christ.


# III

## On the Gifts of the Wise Men

"Behold, there came wise men from the East … and opening their treasures, they offered him gifts."[236]

**W**e seem to expect that, as on other feasts, so also on this day's solemnity, we should have some explanation of the mystery we commemorate. There are other days when we may very usefully speak on sin and vice; but on festival days, and especially on the greater festivals, it is preferable to dwell on what relates to the solemnity, that the mind may be enlightened and the affections also may be aroused. For how are we to solemnize what we are ignorant of, and how shall we know what preachers have not declared? Therefore let not the learned think it irksome if we comply with the demands of charity, and say a few words to those less instructed.

This day's festival, then, takes its name from the apparition of the star: Epiphany means appearance. To-day we celebrate still more definitely the appearance or manifestation of our Lord; and not one only, but three manifestations, as our fathers have transmitted to us. To-day our little King, a few days after His birth, appeared by means of a star to the Magi,

---

236 Matthew 2:1, 11

the first-fruits of the Gentile world. On this day also He went to the Jordan to be baptized, and was there revealed to men by the testimony of God the Father. To-day, likewise, having been invited with His disciples to a marriage feast where the wine failed, He changed water into wine as a sign of His miraculous power. But the manifestation which took place in His infancy is the most attractive one, and we will consider it more attentively; both because it is a sweeter mystery and the one which is specially taken notice of in this day's liturgy.

To-day we have heard read in the Gospel of the feast that Wise Men came from the East to Jerusalem. With good reason did they come from the East who announced to us the new rising of the Sun of Justice, they who illuminated the whole world with their joyful tidings. Unhappy Judea alone, on the contrary, by hating the light, was plunged into a deeper darkness by the effulgent brightness of the new light; her eyes, already clouded, were more incurably blinded by the flashing radiance of the Eternal Sun.

Let us listen to the words of these Wise Men coming from the East: "Where is he that is born King of the Jews?" What unwavering faith! They have no hesitation. They do not question the fact of His birth, but only inquire where it had taken place. At the mention of the word "King" Herod "was troubled," greatly fearing one who would supplant him in his kingdom. That he should fear is not surprising, but that Jerusalem—the City of God, the Vision of Peace—should be troubled with him is indeed a matter for wonder. Behold, how hurtful a wicked government is whose head seeks to bring subjects to conform to its own evil views! Woe to that State where a Herod reigns! It will without doubt share his impiety, and, like him, be troubled at the tidings of salvation. I trust in God that such a spirit will never reign among us, if, indeed, it has begun to get a footing, which may God forbid. It is the malice of a Herod to oppose and seek to stifle in their birth any rising efforts in the cause of religion, and to take part in what destroys the souls of God's little ones. To do so is to join with Herod in seeking to murder the new-born Saviour.

But let us return to the history of this day's mystery; it will lead us to avoid more carefully the spirit of Herod.

The Magi, pursuing their inquiries concerning the King of the Jews, learnt from the Scribes, whom Herod had assembled, the name of the place marked out by the Prophet Micheas for the birth of Christ, the Saviour of the world. Then, leaving the Jews, "behold, the star which they had seen in the east went before them." This plainly shows that when they eagerly sought for human directions they lost the Divine leading; when they turned to earthly teaching the heavenly portent was withdrawn. But once they had left Herod and his court they were immediately "rejoiced with exceeding great joy."[237] For "the star went before them until it came and stood over where the child was."[238] "And entering into the house, they found the child with Mary his mother, and falling down, they adored him."[239]

---

[237] Matthew 2:10
[238] Matthew 2:10
[239] Matthew 2:10

Whence is this to you, O' holy strangers? We have not found so great faith even in Israel. Is it possible that the mean dwelling of a stable and the poverty of the manger-crib do not shock you? That the sight of the poor Mother and her Infant offers you no stumbling-block? No, the Evangelist says: "Opening their treasures, they offered him gold, frankincense, and myrrh." If they had offered only gold, the poverty of the Mother, and how to provide her with the means of bringing up her Child, might have appeared to be their one consideration. But the myrrh and frankincense, along with the gold, intimate the spiritual nature of their oblation.

Amongst worldly riches gold is looked upon as most precious, and this, by God's grace, we religious offered to our Saviour when, for His name, we heartily left all the substance of this world. Only, having left and utterly despised it, it behoves us to seek and eagerly desire the wealth that is heavenly. In like manner we continue to offer the sweet fragrance of incense, which St. John tells us signifies the prayers of the saints. The Prophet also, in Ps. 140, says: "Let my prayer be directed as incense in thy sight."[240] And in Ecclesiasticus we read: "The prayer of him that humbleth himself shall pierce the clouds, and he will not depart until the Most High behold."[241]

That our prayer may thus rise to God it must have the two wings of contempt of the world and mortification of the flesh.

---

[240] Psalm 140:2
[241] Ecclesiasticus 35:21

Our offering will be a pleasing and acceptable sacrifice when, with gold and incense, we bring also our myrrh. Myrrh is bitter, but it is very useful, and preserves the body from returning to the corruption of sin.

We have so far said a few words which may lead us to imitate the offerings of the Magi; we will now show that each of the manifestations of our Lord is a proof of His Divinity.

"And entering into the house" the Wise Men "found the child with Mary his mother."

First, in His infant form which His Mother was fostering in her virginal bosom is manifested the reality of the flesh which He had assumed; and from the fact that the Holy Child was found with His Mother may it not be inferred that He is true Man and truly the Son of man?

In the second manifestation the voice of the Eternal Father—"This is my beloved Son, in whom I am well pleased"—openly acknowledges our Blessed Lord to be the Son of God—God and Man; as does also the descent of the Holy Ghost upon Him in the visible form of a dove.

In the third manifestation He evidently shows Himself to be God and the Author of nature, whose laws He can change at will.

Let us, then, with our whole hearts, love our Lord Jesus Christ as true Man and our Brother. Let us honour Him as Son of God, and adore Him as truly God. Let us firmly believe in Him, let us surrender ourselves utterly into His keeping, for He is neither wanting in power to save us, since He is true God and the true Son of God, nor in the will to save us, for He is, as it were, one of ourselves, true Man and truly the Son of man. And how could He be inexorable to us Who became a sufferer for love of us?


The End.